PLAYS ONE

Charles Wood

PLAYS ONE

VETERANS

ACROSS FROM THE GARDEN OF ALLAH

OBERON BOOKS

LONDON

CONTENTS

INTRODUCTION

Richard Eyre

You could call Charles Wood a playwright, a poet, and a painter. The playwright speaks for himself on the stage and on the screen; the poet is revealed in the text through the repeated rhythms, the hint of rhyme, the stylised translation of conversation, and in the emergence of an idiosyncratic and obsessional voice; the painter is latent in the stage directions: indelible images of a sandhill and a tank in the desert; a decorated Indian elephant; a small Eurasian girl holding the hand of a Malaysian rubber planter in a clearing in the jungle while a record of a British night-club singer plays on a wind-up gramophone; a moonlit soldier stumbling through a perpetual night under the burden of his full kit, a rough beast slouching towards Bedlam.

The work is not easy to perform. It's hard for actors to find naturalness within dialogue that is so highly distilled and so insistently singular, and it takes time, imagination and confidence to allow his scenes to realise their full potential. There's a remarkable scene in *Jingo* (which I directed unsuccessfully in 1976) at the end of the play: the Brigadier responsible for the failure of the British to defend Singapore demands that an English woman gives him a spanking as punishment. Only after the play had been playing for some weeks was the full potency of this tragi-comic scene realised – the dismal demise of the British Empire, embodied in the child-like demand of an upper-class Englishman to be smacked on his bare bottom with the back of a pearl-handed hair-brush, became eerily touching and uncomfortably resonant.

Charles' writing invariably describes closed societies – the army, the British Empire, the theatre – all having their private languages, their peculiar customs, and all steeped in an irreducible Englishness. But the consuming preoccupation of this humane and gentle man is the activity that devours humanity and gentility: war. As with Wilfred Owen, it is the pity of war that he is concerned with, but it is also the glamour – the weapons, orders, insignia, regalia, shoulder flashes, scarlet tunics, cap badges, ranks, battle honours, regimental history, and the private syntax of men amongst men. And the horror – the mud, the blood, the brains, guts, limbs and lives that get shed in foreign fields far from home. And before the confusion, folly and fear of battle, the strutting neatness, cleanness, pomp, order, hierarchy and absurdity of the soldier's life in peace time.

Charles served for five years with the 17th / 21st Lancers, which provided him with the seam to mine his raw material, but perhaps as importantly both his parents were actors. Like soldiers, actors are veterans of many ill-conceived campaigns, are ever-sceptical of the leaders who have dragged them there and they develop a carapace of wit and covert disdain of their superiors to conceal their fear and their boredom.

Charles' seam is not so much warfare as the profession of soldiering, and the point of being a soldier is to break the ultimate taboo – the point is to destroy the enemy on our behalf, to kill people. This apparently self-evident truth is hidden from the recruit by the seductive panoply of uniforms, gold braid, pipes, drums, marching, medals, and the promise of adventure. Charles writes lovingly of all this but his invariable conclusion is that, for all the chivalry and courage, no war, just or unjust, can be acquitted of bestiality: the means never justify the ends. His indictment of war is invoked like a litany: it isn't worth it, it isn't worth it, it isn't worth it.

He shows how war corrupts all relationships, between country and country, man and man, man and woman, but he also shows how irresistibly alluring it can be to young men and older politicians. There is no contemporary writer who has chronicled the experience of modern war with so much authority, knowledge, compassion, wit and despair, and there is no contemporary writer who has received so little of his deserved public acclaim.

John Osborne has always been credited with changing the course of British drama with *Look Back In Anger*, a play that now seems, for all its abrasive, self-lacerating, iconoclastic rhetoric, to look back, not in anger, but with a fiercely desperate nostalgia. If John Osborne was always looking forward to the past, Charles Wood has always looked the present in the face through the prism of the decline of the British Empire, the legacy of the First World War, the vainglory of the Falklands War, or the immutable stalemate of Northern Ireland.

John Osborne and Charles were friends, both actors, both half in love with the tatty shabbiness of backstage life. If I had to make an unenviable choice between the two of them, I would say that it was Charles who has been responsible for the theatrical revolution, but one that has barely begun to take place. The best play to emerge in the Nineties, in my view, is Tony Kushner's *Angels in America*. It is fearlessly ambitious in form and in content, in its refusal to accept the conventions of naturalism – in speech and in staging. In form it attempts everything that Charles attempted in his play about the Indian Empire *H* in the '60s, but Charles was unlucky: he was ahead of his time, and he never found the collaborators who could match the breadth of his epic vision.

I can't help feeling guilty that I haven't done more to argue the case for Charles' work in the theatre, which is the only court that means anything to a playwright. Why? Fashion and faint-heartedness, I suppose; his subject matter is so uncompromisingly painful and tells such uncomfortable truths about mankind – or at least about men. I did direct a film of a screenplay of his: *Tumbledown*, about the Falklands War. A friend of mine sent me a letter he'd received from a distinguished military historian complaining about the film. "I am all for attacking the establishment," said the letter, "but I am choosy about who does it." I'm choosy too, and I am grateful that Charles has been there to challenge and disturb the orthodoxies and theologies of those who sent soldiers to war, and to chronicle the suffering, the stoicism, the heroism and the folly, not only of those who have done the fighting, but also those who have had to pick up the pieces afterwards.

London 1997

VETERANS

or

Hairs in the Gates of the Hellespont

Characters

SIR GEOFFREY KENDLE
MR LAURENCE D'ORSAY (DOTTY)
URSULA MARJORIBANKS
RODNEY
YASHA
PENELOPE D'ORSAY
BRYAN DAVID
BERNIE THE VOLT
TREVOR HOLLINGSHEAD

VETERANS was first performed at The Royal Court Theatre, produced by Michael Codron, on 9th March 1972, with the following cast:

SIR GEOFFREY KENDLE, John Gielgud

MR LAURENCE D'ORSAY (DOTTY), John Mills

URSULA MARJORIBANKS, Jane Evers

RODNEY, Gordon Jackson

YASHA, Ahmed Khalil

PENELOPE D'ORSAY, Ann Bell

BRYAN DAVID, Frank Grimes

BERNIE THE VOLT, Bob Hoskins

TREVOR HOLLINGSHEAD, James Bolam

DIRECTION: Ronald Eyre

DESIGN: Voytek

ACT ONE

Scene 1

The ruined city of Priene in Turkey, 1969.

1969. The curtain rises.

The cavea of a small amphitheatre in the city. Neat rows of stone seats for neat Greek bottoms. At row ten they vanish into unexcavated rubble, scrub, and earth scratchings. Beyond the scrub belt there is a gentle smother of grass and bushes until stone again where a cliff rises sheer. The theatre is very tiny, more of a cockpit. In the front row there are five stone thrones with gougings for fingers, and in the centre there is an altar to Dionysus. There is no sky to be seen as a line or a view of blue.

Discovered, two old men in deckchairs.

The cutain comes down again.

While the curtain is down.
Military music.
Gunfire, drums and bugles, the din of battle joined by horse and foot.
Opening credit titles on screen or curtain with names of actors over scenes of Indian Mutiny carnage.

Scene 2

The curtain rises.

Scene the same. Discovered, two old men in chairs of the type taken on campaign

and location and known as canvas camp-
chairs. The old gentlemen wear faded blue
uniforms of the British Army 1857. Their
swords, complete with scabbards and belts
are stuck in the ground at the side of the
chairs. The old gentlemen sit with their
chins sunk into their chests, their legs
at full stretch, their ankles crossed.

SIR GEOFFREY KENDLE has the crimson ribbon
and suspended military badge of the C.B.
at his throat. He wears a straw hat. His
companion, MR LAURENCE D'ORSAY, is a small
and thickset man with close cropped white
hair and a scrubby ginger moustache.

SIR GEOFFREY KENDLE blows his nose.

The curtain comes down again.

While the curtain is down.
Gunfire, drums and bugles, the din of
battle joined by horse, foot and elephant.
Opening credit titles on screen or curtain.

Scene 3

The curtain rises.

Scene the same. Discovered, two old gentlemen
in chairs and a WOMAN (URSULA MARJORIBANKS)
lying on a gentle smother of grass with
her skirt pulled up and her knees up,
her legs apart. She wears grey
stockings which are now around her
ankles. Her pantloons are spread near,
to be clearly seen.)

Gunfire, drums and bugles, the sound of
distant battle.

SIR GEOFFREY KENDLE stands up. He buttons
his tunic and girds his sword about him.

SIR GEOFFREY KENDLE: I thought I might see
what is what. Go see what is what. If there
is anything is what.

Exit SIR GEOFFREY KENDLE.
The curtain comes down again.

While the curtain is down.
A scream from the WOMAN. Gunfire, drums
and bugles and the din of battle joined
by horse, foot, elephant and WOMAN.

FILM. Wide screen and colour of an epic
tale of the Indian Mutiny but without
sound and with the clapper board indent.
Badly printed and as seen in rushes.
Opening title 'Veterans'.

Scene 4

The curtain rises.

Scene the same. Discovered, one old man
exposing himself to the WOMAN. Or
rather to her drawers she has left
behind, for she has gone. MR LAURENCE
D'ORSAY freezes, looking over his
shoulder at the rising curtain, eyes
following and anticipating its descent.
The curtain stays up, MR LAURENCE D'ORSAY
is momentarily embarrassed. He turns away
upstage and tidies himself. Picks up a
book that has been dropped. In the book
an envelope. He looks at the envelope
and puts it back into the book, stuffs
the book into one of his large campaign

*pockets and comes back to his chair to
sit down, his sword brought forward
between his knees and upright, his
chin rubbing the hilt reflectively; a
flash of irritation.*

*Enter SIR GEOFFREY KENDLE bloodied,
bowed, dusty, tattered and exhausted,
not at all pleased to find the curtain
where it is.*

SIR GEOFFREY KENDLE: (*Sharply.*) Is this
anything to do with you Laurence, eh, this
impossible up and down business?

MR LAURENCE D'ORSAY: Mmmmmmmmm?

SIR GEOFFREY KENDLE: Irritating nonsense.

MR LAURENCE D'ORSAY: How was it Sir
Geoffrey?

SIR GEOFFREY KENDLE: I shall never get
used to horses, all my years.

*Gunfire. SIR GEOFFREY KENDLE shudders, he
flutters his hand feebly in the direction
of the guns and then composes himself.*

The nimble gunner!
Oh. Oh dear me the nimble gunner.

Poor fellows, they do well to be nimble,
I was myself near dragged like Hector
through shameful field,
through no fault of my own in beastly sort,
I would have been, my sword knot caught
in the wheel of a moving gun...

*He tugs at his sword knot, a handsome
affair of red and gold twisted wire
culminating in a cluster of acorns.*

This thing dangles so bloody sly in
the way of things.

MR LAURENCE D'ORSAY: Cut it off.

SIR GEOFFREY KENDLE: Eh? What do you
say Dotty?

MR LAURENCE D'ORSAY: Cut the damn thing
off if you can't cope.

SIR GEOFFREY KENDLE: Really?

MR LAURENCE D'ORSAY: Yes.

SIR GEOFFREY KENDLE: Yes. It's this question
of being a nuisance do you see? I never
like to be a nuisance, set a precedent, have
the whole British Army as then was tossing
aside their sword knots.

MR LAURENCE D'ORSAY: I can't see
that happening.

SIR GEOFFREY KENDLE: Can't you? No. Altogether
too sensible for that aren't they?

MR LAURENCE D'ORSAY: Cut it off, you'll feel
much happier. I should.

SIR GEOFFREY KENDLE: Would you, would you
Dotty?

MR LAURENCE D'ORSAY: The trick is, you
wrap it or tie it round your wrist.

SIR GEOFFREY KENDLE: Yes. Yes I know, I
know. I do that. I always do that when
fighting or anything, that's so you don't
drop the thing, or anything.
I do that.

MR LAURENCE D'ORSAY: Are you called upon
to do much? I'm sorry, I never know

what anyone does until years afterwards...
Do you do much?

SIR GEOFFREY KENDLE: Fighting? No, no,
not any more. Quite a lot at the beginning
of things... day after miserable day I
walloped about on a carthorse sticking a
sword into astonished people, I can't
honestly say I enjoyed it.

MR LAURENCE D'ORSAY: There you are then.

SIR GEOFFREY KENDLE: Yes, ah, I never had
any trouble then because I made sure it
was wrapped two or three times round my
wrist Dotty, the loose end which dangles
so dangerously I made sure was tucked in my
cuff out of harm's way...

MR LAURENCE D'ORSAY: That's the way.
That's the way.

SIR GEOFFREY KENDLE: But you see I hardly
have it out of its... its...

MR LAURENCE D'ORSAY: Scabbard, scabbard.

SIR GEOFFREY KENDLE: Scabbard now, no, no,
I'm very grateful, seem to do more talking
than fighting... now.

MR LAURENCE D'ORSAY: How is the throat?

SIR GEOFFREY KENDLE: In shreds.
I thought I was a goner Dotty, thought I
was being dragged under that dear
elephant, isn't he a patient beast?
Look at him, he's still out there doing
his bit, apparantly they never will
actually step on you if they can possibly
avoid it... like horses,
but you can't help wondering if they know

you in all that dust and fury,
lost in the labyrinth,
I call him Ajax for obvious reasons;
complete confusion out there, I wonder
we are not all of us dead,
elephants and all,
I'm sure nobody heard a word I said,
damn the dangling thing...

MR LAURENCE D'ORSAY: Let me see.

SIR GEOFFREY KENDLE: Oh would you? Would
you Dotty? I would be so grateful...
Dare I say, a poor thing but my own?

*He laughs and holds out the sword knot
obscenely, laughs again.*

See, that's where it got mangled in the
gun being run off.

*MR LAURENCE D'ORSAY doesn't laugh, he
is sometimes without any sense of humour.*

MR LAURENCE D'ORSAY: It's a very long one.

SIR GEOFFREY KENDLE: I would say that was
the whole problem. A few inches shorter,
I could cope.

MR LAURENCE D'ORSAY: Is it longer than mine?

SIR GEOFFREY KENDLE: Is it?

MR LAURENCE D'ORSAY: It is.

SIR GEOFFREY KENDLE: I think it's meant
to be.

MR LAURENCE D'ORSAY: Do you, do you?
Considerably longer than mine.

SIR GEOFFREY KENDLE: Oh no, no, somewhat...

MR LAURENCE D'ORSAY: Considerably.

SIR GEOFFREY KENDLE: Do you honestly think so?
I can't believe there is anything in it.
Would you think the length had any
significance? You should know these things...
Can you see how to remove it?

MR LAURENCE D'ORSAY: Do what you like with
the bloody thing.

SIR GEOFFREY KENDLE: Come now Dotty, I
doubt there's any malice in it – I suppose
I am that bit more important than you are.

MR LAURENCE D'ORSAY: Look at the length
of it Geoffrey, look at that!

SIR GEOFFREY KENDLE: You see your knot is
silver isn't it? Mine is gold.

MR LAURENCE D'ORSAY: Yes, well you can
take the whole thing off. I shall have it.

SIR GEOFFREY KENDLE: No, no, better not.

MR LAURENCE D'ORSAY: You can have mine,
much shorter for you to wear.

SIR GEOFFREY KENDLE: No, no, somebody is
bound to notice and I'll be in dreadful
trouble, I shall tuck it up somewhere.

MR LAURENCE D'ORSAY: Come along now, give
it to me.

SIR GEOFFREY KENDLE: Willingly Dotty, but
what would I do if somebody noticed?

MR LAURENCE D'ORSAY: In all that dust?

SIR GEOFFREY KENDLE: It is surprising
what does notice, you know that, and those

poor fellows hacking away at each other
get into dreadful trouble if they don't
dress properly. No, I think I ought to
try to manage with it, I'll ask if I can
be kept away from guns... they were
awfully kind about it and made a great
deal of fuss, far too much fuss...

MR LAURENCE D'ORSAY: Very well.
I'm sure I'm entitled to a gold one.

SIR GEOFFREY KENDLE: Very possibly. Young
fellow, what's his name? My son, he's got
one and he's only a lieutenant. Bryan.
I'd let you borrow it. (*His own sword knot
indicated.*)

MR LAURENCE D'ORSAY: No.

SIR GEOFFREY KENDLE: No, wouldn't do.

MR LAURENCE D'ORSAY: (*Looking off right.*) Is
that soldier waving at you or me?

SIR GEOFFREY KENDLE: Oh, oh.

*SIR GEOFFREY KENDLE waves. MR LAURENCE
D'ORSAY looks at him and then off.*

MR LAURENCE D'ORSAY: He's still waving, it
must be for me.

A bugle call. Decision from D'ORSAY.

Yes, it is me.

SIR GEOFFREY KENDLE: You must be wanted on
the field of battle; I'm not in the least
surprised, it's complete chaos, they're
dragging in everybody wears a uniform, oh,
oh dear me... ah, Dotty, ah, is that
your horse there? What a nice quiet horse

it is, not like my nag, a fiend on four
legs, has to have a leg tied up
every time I am called on
to say a few words; still, you don't have
much to say, oh, you know, what I mean, ah yes,
he seems very gentle and considerate, I do like
the look of him...

MR LAURENCE D'ORSAY: I may not be quite
so important as you Geoffrey, Sir Geoffrey,
in regard to the length of the sword knot
I am given, say, or the words I am expected
to speak... but I am an excellent
horseman.

SIR GEOFFREY KENDLE: Oh you are, you are!

MR LAURENCE D'ORSAY: If my mount impresses
you with his manners it is perhaps because
I have schooled him...

SIR GEOFFREY KENDLE: It is, it is, a very
nice old thing.

MR LAURENCE D'ORSAY: ... and not because
he lacks spirit or is too old to be
troublesome...

SIR GEOFFREY KENDLE: No, no, a most perfect
animal – full of mettle, I can see it, I
can see he is a first-rate ride, gives an
impression of gentleness. I know you're a
fine horseman, I've seen you riding about
awfully well and never look like falling off.
Do be careful Dotty, do you see what they
have done to me, have you got any cigarettes?

MR LAURENCE D'ORSAY: No. I haven't.

*Exit MR LAURENCE D'ORSAY snapping his
fingers in the way horsemen do, it*

isn't easy and SIR GEOFFREY KENDLE
can't do it. He rummages in an airline
bag hanging from the back of his
camp-chair, talking the while, looking
for cigarettes that he knows he hasn't
got, paper tissues, newspapers of tissue
for overseas delivery, sun lotion and
cream, oranges, a paperback copy of
'Herodotus', another of Orwell's 'Essays'
('The Decline of the English Murder'),
sunglasses, a few paper cups, aspirin
and bandages, an old box Brownie camera,
boiled sweets in a tin.

SIR GEOFFREY KENDLE: Have you not? Damn,
you see I haven't got any at all, dammit,
what does Penelope smoke, something vile?
Oh, you're gone. After all, soon be over
and we'll all go home.

He dabs sun-cream on his nose, puts
on his sunglasses and his straw hat
and opens his tunic. He then decides
to take his tunic off, stands up and
does so, putting it on the back of
his chair. He is wearing period braces
and underwear. He sits down again and
starts to anoint his arms and neck with
sun lotion, wipes his hands on a paper
tissue and can find nowhere to put the
used tissue. He puts it under a stone
and adds another stone to hide it better,
sits down and doesn't like the stone in
its new position, gets up and moves it,
can then see the tissue, looks for a
better place to hide the tissue, tugs at
a larger stone near the smother of earth
and grass, it comes loose and with it

a shower of used plastic cups. He looks at
the plastic cups sadly, goes back to his
chair and puts the used tissue in his
string bag. He is sweating from his
walk in the sun to find a place to hide
the tissue, dabs his face with more
tissue to mop up the sweat, removes
the cream from his nose,
applies more cream, a large and
ridiculous blob – wipes his hands
and looks for somewhere to put the
used tissue, gives up, exhausted, tosses
it to the ground, and slumps back into his
chair. Then he sits bolt upright,
listens, puts his tunic back on, crosses
his legs and straightens his back, his
straw hat firmly placed on his head. A
moment, he looks desperately in
need of a cigarette again,
he hears someone coming, looks off
and shrinks into his chair
as RODNEY enters.
Enter RODNEY and SIR GEOFFREY KENDLE
looks firmly in the other direction.
RODNEY is too busy flirting with his
friend in the Turkish Cavalry to notice
anyone else.
Enter YASHA, a young trooper of Turkish
Cavalry who stands apart, his hands
crossed in front of him in a curiously
maidenish manner. RODNEY is struggling
with a large hamper which clinks. He
puts the hamper down in the shade of a
tree, puts his hands on his hips and
smiles at YASHA. Takes a small guide book
from inside his shirt.

RODNEY: Supreme, absolutely supreme Yasha.
Your beautiful country is so beautiful,
your heritage,
shall I read you what it says of your
heritage to you,
from a Guide Book given me by a friend,
this is where they had their plays,
them dreadful Greeks you keep hating,
the Royal Box,
now you should not hate the Greeks
because they had some truly lovely ideas,
still do have,
that's the Royal Box then,
and five stone thrones with grooves for
the fingers I see,
they fit, they fit!

He exclaims as he tries his fingers
in the grooves, not sitting in the
throne but bending his body to its
shape. He shouts and leaps into the
air, not high, coming down in an
attitude and pointing.

Look, look, that's the altar to Dionysus,
him... him as was lovely,
ooooooooooooh at night,
I can feel it now,
hear them flutes and cymbals and all
of us stoned magic,
supreme,
slip back here tonight Yasha,
you and me and some friends and some of
that lovely hasha, Yasha, to say us
prayers, do you think so? Shall you be
able to come if I speak nicely to your
sergeant?
Do say you shall.

Supreme though, absolutely supremely
situate for a picnic,
quite by to the location
and shaded for their old heads, my
old gentlemen,
don't, don't look at me I know I'm
going don't I? No, don't, the sun's shine
is cruel on a pink head and I get no
protection from my fair colour,
letters for them.

*He crosses to the deckchairs, doing
an obvious dancer strut,
strikes an attitude halfway, holding
a bundle of letters and looking back
at YASHA. SIR GEOFFREY KENDLE is
shrinking into the deckchair in an
agony of embarrassment, holding up his
feet and holding down his head in the
hope that he will not be noticed.*

You didn't know I used to be a dancer
did you? Well, not your fault,
first intimation I have given you,
mind you I am stiffed up,
I thought the sun would waken me my
bones, what do you want then,
a demi plie?

*He does one, and then stands over
the deckchairs,
sorting the letters.*

Where they will sit, my old men, and
letters for them,
one for you, one for you, one for you,
one for him, two for you, three for you,
one for you,oooooooooooooh and one each
from the same source...

*Flicking the letters over the top
of the deckchairs, a few for MR LAURENCE
D'ORSAY on one chair and a pile for
SIR GEOFFREY KENDLE.*

... dear Alexander Ltd has one
each to them, to Sir Geoffrey Kendle,
To Mr Laurence D'Orsay,
same size, same weight, same bendy,
same day of posting,
a script,
for both of them, the same, oh Sandy Ltd is
naughty – there will be RUCTIONS! I
Can't wait.

*He drops the letters (packages) and embraces
the atmosphere. SIR GEOFFREY KENDLE
looks at the large package on the
ground in front of him,
at an identical package on the chair
next to him. He reaches out a hand
to take the package and pulls it back
quickly when RODNEY exclaims:*

Truly, truly, truly wonderful a place to
set down things for a picnic,
fruit and chicken, pieces of veal
in plastic bags,
hardly boiled eggs,
champagne and Kavak,
cushions and Sunday papers for a day
in a setting!

*SIR GEOFFREY nearly falls from his chair,
trying to reach his package without
being seen by RODNEY.*

Oh Sir Geoffrey!
I was just going to say... I was going

to say how very Uncle Vanya!
And there you are!

SIR GEOFFREY KENDLE: Am I?

RODNEY: Isn't it though, isn't it Chekhov
to the T, Tchekhov?
Supreme.

SIR GEOFFREY KENDLE: Quite wonderful.

*He quavers, as RODNEY advances on him
with a purposeful strut.
Gunfire.
RODNEY stops in his tracks, and leaps
clean out of his skin,
coming down to earth in an attitude
with his eyes rolling.*

RODNEY: I wish to gawd they would not let
off like that, I near shit myself.
Attitude cacky tights.

*Holding his trousers off
with finger and thumb, looking at YASHA
who is smiling broadly.*

Oh very friends of Covent Garden, you
can laugh,
look at him laughing Sir Geoffrey.

A bugle call has RODNEY jump again.

There they go again,
oh it is spoiling, you want to hear the
bees buzzing don't you, I mean, such a place as this...?
Isn't it wonderful? Supreme?

*SIR GEOFFREY KENDLE cannot bring
himself to go,
much as he would like to, he sinks
back into his chair.*

SIR GEOFFREY KENDLE: Are we going to eat
   lunch here, is that the intention?

RODNEY: Well. It's supreme isn't it?

SIR GEOFFREY KENDLE: Oh supreme, very nice,
   superb, quite wonderful, have you got a
   cigarette?

   He asks regretfully,
   he would obviously rather not ask the
   obvious RODNEY for anything.
   RODNEY is delighted to be of service,
   with a cork tip, thrust at SIR GEOFFREY.

   Thank you, thank
   you very much Rodney. I am grateful, I
   can't think where I have put mine.

RODNEY: You've had them thieved.

SIR GEOFFREY KENDLE: Have I?

RODNEY: They're all thieves, like Ali Baba.

SIR GEOFFREY KENDLE: Are they, are they?

   RODNEY is sitting alongside
   SIR GEOFFREY and taking his shoes off.

RODNEY: Have you noticed, such hurtful grass
   they grow in Turkey, gets in your socks,
   have you experienced it Sir Geoffrey? You
   won't have, not in your boots. Like needles.
   Don't be tempted to go about in pumps
   whatever you do, my socks is full of little
   burrs just that way up from the jeep. Don't
   they cling though? Worse than bleeding Turks.
   Look at him standing there thick as mutton...
   Look at
   him with his bangle on his wrist, you
   would not think he was a soldier

would you? Look at him, me and my
shadow, follows me everywhere.

SIR GEOFFREY KENDLE: You're quite
outrageous Rodney.

RODNEY: Don't! Oh I do want him.

SIR GEOFFREY KENDLE: Lovely day.

RODNEY: Isn't it lovely to talk dirty
to them, they don't understand a flaming
word!
Look at him looking all lost
with a face on him long as his horse.
Look.

SIR GEOFFREY KENDLE: Do you ride at all
Rodney? I don't suppose you get time
do you? What with catering for all our
needs, I mean, food... providing food.

RODNEY: Oh love, I don't.

SIR GEOFFREY KENDLE: Would you like to?
Why don't you, now?

RODNEY: I would Sir Geoffrey, I would
like to only my legs are too short.
Exquisite shy aren't they, horses?
Some of them look very kind and natural
don't they? Only they can turn, horses,
can't they? What happens should you be
sat on board an *at* and it turns?

SIR GEOFFREY KENDLE: Sat on what?

RODNEY: Sat on an *at*. *At*. Turkish for
horse. Hence you get Yasha called an
at-minder and such as *at*-fly, *at*-shit...

SIR GEOFFREY KENDLE: Yes, yes of course.
I'm sure I didn't know.

RODNEY: You have to have some words.

SIR GEOFFREY KENDLE: I find if I shout
    at them in German...

RODNEY: You don't.

SIR GEOFFREY KENDLE: Yes.

RODNEY: You mean thing. Fancy shouting at
    your patient old *at* in nasty German...

SIR GEOFFREY KENDLE: Oh he's a terrible
    old thing, I call him the terrible Turk.

RODNEY: Ssssssssssssh! For fear of offence! (*Warningly.*)

SIR GEOFFREY KENDLE: Actually I think he's
    a lady.

RODNEY: Aaaaaah, poor old cow.

SIR GEOFFREY KENDLE: I'm sure you would
    enjoy riding, Rodney, did you but try.
    I don't.

RODNEY: I mean I wouldn't know which string
    to pull should it turn... only they can
    turn and toss you off, can't they Yasha?
    I mean everybody loves a horse, but...
    Did you happen to be out the other day
    when half of the Brirish Army took a turn
    and bolted straight back to the barracks
    with their little Turks hanging on like
    grim death? Like the clappers with
    Turks dropping off like lumps of cack!
    Grim death dear,
    I'm glad Yasha was off with toothache,
    it wasn't funny, I nearly pissed myself.
    But not funny for their mothers,
    they're only conscripts you know. Of
    course they are bred to it, I mean up

on the top of an *at* before they can walk
aren't they? And their mothers,
why they're so bandy – no, no I would
like to say I had had the experience because
they are such graceful animals aren't they?
I would like to if they could find me a
wooden one. I mean, I do like to see other
people on them, jumping on the telly with
Thing on them,
they're lovely creatures,
with Thing winning things over the jumps
and those junior soldiers putting them
back when they go clonk, I adore all that.
Yasha rides well,
ever so straight he is,
he was born on an *at* wasn't you Yasha,
why he's so graceful, look at his eyes
just like a horse's eyes, such pools, I
could go get my trunks and dive straight
in! Don't!
Here she is then, madame.

He looks off and anticipates the
entrance of PENELOPE, a nod.

No, I would go for a ride on a horse
if Yasha would find me a nice one,
with its legs tied up,
the way they do
for you, your moments of high drama,
they do, now don't say they don't look
after you.

SIR GEOFFREY KENDLE: Oh they do, they are
forced to do.

Enter PENELOPE during this, she stands
on the edge of the orchestra
looking at the stones and the yellow

grass growing in the cracks, walks
into the centre of the orchestra
shifting the sunglasses on her nose,
squinting into the impossible sky on
the ball of one foot for moment. She
is dressed n swirls of purple, green,
blue silk georgette, very little of it,
showing breasts, legs, navel, glimpses of
hair. She is expensive,
and, though this always comes as a
surprising afterthought, she is not
beautiful. She watches an eagle float
in the sky directly overhead.

RODNEY: Don't say good morning or anything.

She doesn't, she doesn't say anything.
She smiles at YASHA, who grins and
shuffles his feet shyly,
worry beads dancing through his
clasping fingers.

SIR GEOFFREY KENDLE: Penelope, thank goodness.
So you did get out.

SIR GEOFFREY KENDLE stands up to
greet her, he is overwhelmed with
gratitude, nearly tramples RODNEY down
to reach her, stands off some way from
her. PENELOPE kisses him on the cheek
and looks up into the sky again.

PENELOPE: An eagle.

SIR GEOFFREY KENDLE: Thank goodness.

PENELOPE: Why?

SIR GEOFFREY KENDLE: Why?

PENELOPE: I've never seen an eagle flying before,
actually flying. I hope it is an eagle.

Look Geoffrey, can you see it?
Why do you thank goodness to see me?

SIR GEOFFREY KENDLE: Oh, oh I'm sitting here
all alone, as it were...

PENELOPE: Rodney.

RODNEY: Yes, he does mean me.

PENELOPE: Good morning.

SIR GEOFFREY KENDLE: Oh dear, bang go my
kippers.

RODNEY: Never! I'm not that sort of cook.
You'll get your kippers Sir Geoffrey.

SIR GEOFFREY KENDLE: I'm always doing it, I
did it to Dotty just before he went off, said
a dreadful thing, some dreadful things.
Dotty was here Penny, he has gone off to do
some acting, he said to tell you.

PENELOPE: Gone off to do some acting has he?
Well, there alway has to be a first time.

SIR GEOFFREY KENDLE: Oh come now, he is
often very good – you are unkind about your
husband.

PENELOPE: Am I?
You know, I stopped having a husband
after the first one.

SIR GEOFFREY KENDLE: I get that heavy
feeling in the pit of my stomach
when I hear you say such things, Carole
used to say things like that, she was
such an unhappy girl, Carole, when...

PENELOPE: Would you say that it was an eagle
up there?

*SIR GEOFFREY KENDLE looks up into the
sky, puts his hand across his brow to
shade his eyes even though he does
wear sunglasses. He continues.*

SIR GEOFFREY KENDLE: When she was married. Do you
know Carole?

And then he sneezes.

I can't see a thing without these sunglasses,
they make me sneeze. Is it a big bird?
If it is a big bird, really big bird is it?
Must be an eagle. Do they have eagles
in Turkey? Why not?

*Sneezing again, looking away and
lifting his sunglasses up on his brow
he says:*

No I shouldn't go looking in the sky for
fear of conjunctivitis. It is an eagle,
big bird like that.

PENELOPE: Did you see it?

SIR GEOFFREY KENDLE: If it's a big bird.
Look, come and sit down and show me your
black eye. Have Dotty's chair.

*RODNEY gets to his feet quickly and
says pointedly:*

RODNEY: Yes, I am going.

SIR GEOFFREY KENDLE: (*Charmingly.*) Are you
Rodney? Thank goodness... I mean, some
where for Mrs D'Orsay to sit.

PENELOPE: Are you sure Rodney?

RODNEY: You are kind. You haven't got a
black eye. She hasn't got a black eye.

Passing under her and looking up at
her face as he passes,
to stand some way off, looking from
PENELOPE to YASHA to SIR GEOFFREY and
back again to PENELOPE. He comes back.

SIR GEOFFREY KENDLE: I am pleased Penelope
darling, good.

RODNEY: No, no I tell a lie, she has got
one, I see it now. (*Peering.*)

PENELOPE: Yes, I have.

SIR GEOFFREY KENDLE: Oh dear I am sorry.

RODNEY: (*From behind his hand, indicating YASHA.*)
He's looking at you darling, you've
disturbed him, Yasha.

PENELOPE: Yes I'm sure.

RODNEY: I think it's dreadful the way
you girls shamefully expose yourself. They've
never seen anything like it,
these boys,
can you wonder you get raped?

PENELOPE: Speak for yourself.

RODNEY: Oh it has happened.

PENELOPE: Has it?

RODNEY: Not me dear – I do not believe in
force, never needed it, not after the
first time anyway, that can get a bit
tense – no, Dina the costume lady.

PENELOPE: Oh.

RODNEY: Yes, haven't you heard?

PENELOPE: No.

RODNEY: Oh, well, seems she was walking
   one day in her mini skirt,
   her mouth full of safety pins,
   when bold as brass, not thinking, she
   goes to put a tuck in the kilt of a
   seeming perfectly respectable Turkish
   Highlander of the British Army as then was,
   into the midst of them, vanished, not
   seen again for hours...

While RODNEY launches into his story,
PENELOPE listens and watches YASHA,
SIR GEOFFREY KENDLE slumps back into
his chair; they both listen in silence
and without amusement.

... comes out the other end on her knees
and out of her mind,
having been tossed from the one to the
other it seems,
from finger to Turkish finger; she was
speechless. I don't know what she expected,
they're treating it as rape,
oh yes,
but you can't blame the boys can you? I
mean, what sort of a life is it out all
weathers on horses?
Of course they're going to feel it
aren't they? I mean wouldn't you if it
was there, so to speak?
She was shattered apparently,
poor love,
she's just got over the shock of her
husband, poor love, he's given up and
she came out here to forget... whether
or no, she's in trousers this morning
under sedation,
she loved it really except she had a bit

of a headache, everybody came to see her
and say how sorry,
did you go? She's intimated she'll go on,
did you go and see her?

*No response from PENELOPE or SIR GEOFFREY
KENDLE although PENELOPE might be giggling,
RODNEY is not pleased but continues.*

No, I didn't go.
I didn't know, nobody told me. I'd have
loved to have gone and said how sorry,
nobody told me,
like nobody told me about that poor boy
from Huddersfield languishing in a
Turkish nick,
did you know? I didn't, I'd have loved
to have gone to see him. She's said
she'll go on,
she could have had a rest of course and
done the ironing,
have you seen how it's piling up after
that dip in the Ganges, dirty river, as was,
but she wouldn't have it... she's out
this morning bold as brass,
she's a very brave girl is our Dina; I'll
say that for the British Army as is, she'd have
been totally ignored in Knightsbridge no
matter what she wore.

*Annoyed by the lack of response,
RODNEY asks loudly of PENELOPE:*

Was it you asked me for sausages?
Mrs D'Orsay?

PENELOPE: I'm sorry?

RODNEY: Yes it was.

PENELOPE: Oh!

RODNEY: Yes. Only they're held up in Beirut
   by Walls, so you'll have to make do with
   what you've got!

   So saying he sweeps out. In dudgeon.
   Exit RODNEY followed by YASHA.
   Silence for a moment and then SIR
   GEOFFREY KENDLE asks:

SIR GEOFFREY KENDLE: Sausages?

PENELOPE: I'm awfully bored with kebab, I
   never want to see another skewer.

SIR GEOFFREY KENDLE: You know my kippers
   come from Beirut by Pan Am, it's terribly
   sweet of Rodney to arrange it,
   I'm heartily sick of kippers, isn't he a
   loathesome little man, so queer!
   That's why I said thank goodness when
   you arrived, still, if he's getting you
   your sausages.

PENELOPE: I've yet to see one.

SIR GEOFFREY KENDLE: Took an awful long
   time for me to get my kippers, I
   never want to see another.
   He does rub it in, boxes of them.
   What you must do is get a steak for that
   eye, now who was it had a T-bone steak,
   did you see someone flaunting a T-bone
   steak the other night? Apparently you can
   get them from the American P.X. place,
   if you want to saddle yourself with an
   American, now who was it had one?
   Never mind.
   Is it still there, your eagle?

PENELOPE: Yes, it's still there.

SIR GEOFFREY KENDLE: I really must get
some better sunglasses, might I try yours?

*PENELOPE gives him her sunglasses. She has
a black eye, not very bad, just a slight
discolouration. SIR GEOFFREY KENDLE looks
through the sunglasses and shakes his head,
hands them back to her.*

Can you really see through these?

PENELOPE: Yes, of course.

SIR GEOFFREY KENDLE: Oh you are vain!
Penelope, you must be terribly shortsighted.

PENELOPE: I am.

SIR GEOFFREY KENDLE: I knew you were; all
you girls are nowadays, that's why your
scenes are so good in close;
here, have them back, they make me feel
quite queasy... you are all of you
blind as bats and acting us off the screen
with your marvellous intensity,
searing intensity;
and it's simply because you have to
concentrate extraordinarily hard to keep
from bumping into things. Those marvellous
love scenes you do – you haven't the faintest
idea who you are talking to, where you are
standing or what piece of equipment is about
to swing down and hit you, I wonder most of
all how you find your marks.

PENELOPE: We feel them with our toes.

SIR GEOFFREY KENDLE: Do you? Do you? So do
I – it is the only way actually.
Now I see your precious eagle, isn't he

large! Oh I am glad not to be a tortoise.
Have you seen any of the rushes?

PENELOPE: No.

SIR GEOFFREY KENDLE: No, better not.
Does Dotty like you to see his scenes?

PENELOPE: No.

SIR GEOFFREY KENDLE: No, quite right.

PENELOPE: He's dreadful.

SIR GEOFFREY KENDLE: What? Oh no, no.
Oh he is a big one, your eagle. Have they
not been known to carry off sheep, not
to say what they might drop, didn't one
of them drop Sinbad? No, that was a roc,
was it not? And poor serious Aeschylus...
Oh yes, whole sheep.

PENELOPE: The only sheep around here are in khaki.

SIR GEOFFREY KENDLE: I do feel sorry for
them, the poor soldiers. Do you see what
they are given to eat?
My groom is so sweet. I gave him a bar
of chocolate for coping with Arkle the
fiend. Should one?

PENELOPE: Mine seems to function on fags.

SIR GEOFFREY KENDLE: I'm not sure that
one should.

PENELOPE: The only thing you're not
supposed to do is give them money.

SIR GEOFFREY KENDLE: Oh I don't.

PENELOPE: Do you know they get tickets to
the brothel – once a month or so.

SIR GEOFFREY KENDLE: Really?

PENELOPE: My disgusting husband has been.

SIR GEOFFREY KENDLE: Where?

PENELOPE: It's called The Compound, he says he only went to look.

SIR GEOFFREY KENDLE: I'm sure he did only go to look..

PENELOPE: So am I.

SIR GEOFFREY KENDLE: Never mind. Darling have you got any? I had the most dreadful experience this morning. I won't tell you about it, but have you got a cigarette?

PENELOPE: Darling, I'm not smoking.

SIR GEOFFREY KENDLE: I didn't bring any.

PENELOPE: Really. I'm not smoking.

SIR GEOFFREY KENDLE: Oh but you are!

PENELOPE: No, I'm not.

SIR GEOFFREY KENDLE: Surely you are!

PENELOPE: I'm not love, I'm not, I'm awfully sorry... I've stopped.

SIR GEOFFREY KENDLE: Are you sure?

PENELOPE: I stopped, ages ago.

SIR GEOFFREY KENDLE: Oh, you see, oh shit!

PENELOPE: Love, I'm so sorry.

SIR GEOFFREY KENDLE: Ah.

Dejected, he sinks back into his chair, rummages in his string bag

for his tin of boiled sweets,
opens the tin, pops a sweet into his
mouth and then, apologizing, offers
the tin to PENELOPE who shakes her head.

PENELOPE: So much better for you.

She giggles. He dolefully sucks his
sweet and looks at the package, the
large envelope amongst his letters,
at the similar envelope on the chair
next to him.

SIR GEOFFREY KENDLE: I don't like opening
mail, I shall not open these awhile, I must
say that I would never object to my wife
opening my letters if I had a wife...

PENELOPE: Do you know anything about Greek
theatres Geoffrey?

SIR GEOFFREY KENDLE: Everything.

With a sigh,
such a sigh says the topic is dead.
It isn't, PENELOPE makes a moue and is
determinedly continuing, leaning back
into the warmth of the stone throne,
enjoying it.

PENELOPE: Like lying back in a warm bath. Do
you think they intended it to be?

SIR GEOFFREY KENDLE: I'm sure.
They were insatiably sensual, still are.

PENELOPE: Greeks?

SIR GEOFFREY KENDLE: No, the orchestra
stalls.

Holding the large envelope/package
addressed boldly 'SIR GEOFFREY KENDLE'

*in his left hand he picks up the other
envelope/package addressed 'MR LAURENCE
D'ORSAY' weighing them, comparing them.*

Was a time you could tell, Monday morning,
a part was a part then. What has Fanny Craddock
got for us to eat, to drink, to drink?

PENELOPE: It is the absolute right name for
   him, Fanny.

SIR GEOFFREY KENDLE: I thought so.

PENELOPE: In the American sense meaning his bum.

SIR GEOFFREY KENDLE: He does rather, in the
   Chaucerian sense, rather hang it out the
   window to be kissed.

PENELOPE: Uuuuuuugh! In the English sense
   meaning he's a twat.

SIR GEOFFREY KENDLE: Whatever sense, whatever
   you do don't you go getting blisters on
   yours, will you?

PENELOPE: The least of my worries.

SIR GEOFFREY KENDLE: Well come and sit
   here in a cool chair, Dotty's chair,
   before you do, sitting on hot stone. I
   think you should come and open your
   husband's mail just this once,
   you'll thank me for it afterwards.
   What a lot of letters to open and Dotty
   so busy in the thick of it.
   A script. I expect I've had this one
   before. What I do is, 'not known at this
   address', 'gone away',
   I get one almost every day,
   they're always dropping through the
   letter box, plays,

such a lot of people are writing plays,
they're all awfully good.
This one is fromAlexander, he really should
know better;
sometimes I do one,
always the wrong one it turns out;
if I open it and I do when I'm feeling
unwanted, I have a method, I make a
tiny mark on the title page,
you see you never know, I find them all
masterpieces,
what I do is make a mark and if it comes
back three times I know they really want
me and I do it.
What does Dotty do?

PENELOPE: Do you like lizards?

SIR GEOFFREY KENDLE: I think he ought to
do it. Look, he's got one. Does he have
much sent him these days?

PENELOPE: Who?

SIR GEOFFREY KENDLE: Dotty.

PENELOPE: What?

SIR GEOFFREY KENDLE: Plays sent him to read.

PENELOPE: I don't know.

SIR GEOFFREY KENDLE: Do you not?

PENELOPE: Hardly any.

SIR GEOFFREY KENDLE: Then I think he ought
to do it. Does he have a method?

PENELOPE: I expect he counts his lines.

SIR GEOFFREY KENDLE: First-rate method
except you can't help reading them. He

must be frightfully disappointed with
this film, he had quite a lot of very
good lines to begin with.

PENELOPE: Until Trevor found he couldn't
say them.

SIR GEOFFREY KENDLE: I think he says them
awfully well, when he remembers them. It
can't be easy, he rides awfully well.
It can't be easy to do both.

*PENELOPE doesn't answer. She leans back
under the sun and suddenly pushes
out an arm to point, saying:*

PENELOPE: There's another.

SIR GEOFFREY KENDLE: What?

PENELOPE: There's one, see?

SIR GEOFFREY KENDLE: Oh yes.

PENELOPE: Aren't they still?

SIR GEOFFREY KENDLE: Darling, they're all
over the place.
What are you doing?

*PENELOPE is pulling up her skirt and
lifting it, flapping it.*

Is there anyone looking?

PENELOPE: I don't know. Do you not like them,
lizards?

SIR GEOFFREY KENDLE: Like them?
Oh I can't say, do people like them, I mean
are they fancied, lizards?
I suggest your eagle might fancy them,
your precious eagle,

poor old thing he probably dotes on
lizards, has them on toast. Lizard canapés.
Penelope, are you aware that their tails
come off?
I thought I'd warn you, they leave their
tails behind.
Lizards. I much prefer them to horses.

PENELOPE: I don't, I love horses.

SIR GEOFFREY KENDLE: Do you? No, not my
favourite animal, the horse.

PENELOPE: You can't mean it.

SIR GEOFFREY KENDLE: Yes, I do mean it, and
they know it.

PENELOPE: What about my lovely Benjy, don't
you like Benjy?

SIR GEOFFREY KENDLE: I do. I like him
very much, nice old thing. Is he fit
for this life?

PENELOPE: I love my darling Benjy.

SIR GEOFFREY KENDLE: He never looks awfully
well to me, is he? I suppose he is a horse.

PENELOPE: He's a lovely old thing.

SIR GEOFFREY KENDLE: Like that eagle, poor
old bird, get close to him you'll probably
find his feathers are dropping out,
like everything else in Turkey,
never turn it over with the toe of your
boot...
Darling do put your dress down, all these
soldiers about.

PENELOPE: I can cope.

SIR GEOFFREY KENDLE: I'm sure you can.
I should hate to be trampled in the rush,
that's all. I'm very worried about
your behaviour.
I recognize the symptoms.

PENELOPE: Do you?

SIR GEOFFREY KENDLE: Are you coming to sit
here? Let me move these things for you,
letters and things,
then you can pull your skirt down and
sit like a young lady...

PENELOPE: I'm only getting some sun to my
legs, really, you are an old woman.

SIR GEOFFREY KENDLE: They ought to
be answered, these letters. This one looks
very important, should you not set to and
answer it?
Dotty is a brute.

*PENELOPE comes over to the chair,
SIR GEOFFREY KENDLE looking carefully
at her black eye,
he lifts up her sunglasses as she
sits and turns to thank him for
removing the letters;
he holds them in his hand and tosses
them into her lap when she is sitting.*

I'm sorry, it was wrong of me to
mention your black eye in front of the
frightful Rodney.

PENELOPE: Never mind.
Is it awful?

SIR GEOFFREY KENDLE: But I did want to
know because you looked so distressed
last night.

PENELOPE: It feels awful.

SIR GEOFFREY KENDLE: It looks quite nice.

PENELOPE: Rubbish.

SIR GEOFFREY KENDLE: I think it suits you.
I like it. The merest smudge of blue,
a smudge of vulnerability,
a thumb-print of brutality,
the merest smudge I promise you, but
you've seen it,
this morning, what was it like this
morning?
You know I find you beautiful, not
beautiful, you're not beautiful, you
are... oh,
beautiful will do but it won't you know.
He is such a brute, your husband.
He used his first two most shamefully,
his first wife had eyes large as buttons
and a frightened mouth,
a pretty little thing, had a hat. I
grew very fond of her. We had a terrible
time with Dotty as you can imagine,
mooning about the theatre sobbing he was
not fit to buckle her shoes,
or unbuckle,
or whatever he did,
or wanted to do. Oh you know the sort
of thing, you know Dotty,
perhaps he doesn't do it now? Pretty
little thing, She struck everybody as
being very pretty... darling I do
ask you to take the gratest care of that
fly because should it come to bite you,
you'll have the most frightful swelling.

He flaps at the fly,
a limp and ineffectual gesture.

I don't think I like Dotty. I have never
really liked him.
You must have, no?
Did you not ever? Not in the least?
Oh poor Dotty!
I often think he might hit me. Well, that
was his first wife,
did you ever meet her? No reason why you
should, it was longer ago than I care to
remember. Pretty little thing, Dotty
quite went over,
she did marry again... to an actor,
oh a long time after Dotty,
dreadful,
in distressing circumstances outside his
house, a lamp-post.
Are you sure? You must have had some
regard for the poor devil... liked him
a little, he can be very good looking
when he likes.
No?
Actually, I know, I've known him for forty
years and I can never be sure he is
not going to hit me.
He never has.
I have never been hit. There are people
are hit and those that go about hitting,
and those there are that hit it off with
neither, the one attracts the other,
hitter to happily hit,
perhaps,
oh, perhaps not... I mean, you are
probably innocent of any desire to be
bashed about. I'm sure I'm wrong.

*Confused, he picks up his mail and
sifts through his letters,*

not liking any of them,
and showing it. PENELOPE grins at him.

PENELOPE: You've done it again Sir G.

SIR GEOFFREY KENDLE: I know.

PENELOPE: You never want to hit me.

SIR GEOFFREY KENDLE: Oh, oh, no.

PENELOPE: Do you?

SIR GEOFFREY KENDLE: Not actually hit.
I often think Dotty would hit less if he
had a few more,
hits... oh I know he did all those
stiff upper lip things and station platform
things with the girls early on,
tremendously successful, and *Target for*
Tonight was a feather in his cap,
everybody noticed him in it, *F for Freddie,*
one of our aircraft is missing,
D for Dotty... was he in *Target for Tonight?*
Oh lor, do you know I don't believe he was,
there you are you see, that goes to show
how easy it is to slip up on a stiff upper lip.
I was rarely asked.
But Dotty was, he did all those things
superbly... a born captain,
he got a real Military Cross you know.
I don't know what we would have said
without him, those follow-my-leader days.
The awful truth?
I never knew it.

PENELOPE: Were you never asked to take a
little boat to Dunkirk or anything?

SIR GEOFFREY KENDLE: Once.
By dear Alexander who knew how at a loose

end I felt and suggested I might like to
read for *The Art of Camouflage*,
a property dear to him at the time; he
spent his days resplendently camouflaged
as a colonel of a most posh regiment,
one of those that insists on its badge
being as small as is decent and calls
itself by a number oblique number rather
than the name everybody knows it by... I
was up for The Voice of Camouflage in Nature
which went all through,
and I could have built it you see, it could
have led to almost anything in future
instalments... I was ecstatic, I sped
from Alexander's ghastly cubbyhole under the
stairs somewhere grand and guarded, straight
round to Carole to tell her,
demanding she should lead me by the hand
into her garden... but it came to nothing,
not dear Carole's fault.
Two days in Oswestry draped in shrimp net
and nettles, and yards of hessian loop,
with fantastic garlands did she come,
of crow flowers, nettles, daisies and long
purples...

PENELOPE: ... that liberal sheperds call hot
cocks, not hollyhocks.

SIR GEOFFREY KENDLE: Yes. Anyway, my Voice
of Camouflage in Nature was wrong the
sergeant said. He was kind and apologetic
and had seen my Richard but my voice was
wrong, I did too much...
I slunk from Oswestry at dead of night I
was so upset. Utterly ashamed.
They gave it to a marvelous little

man who played the lead in *Where Do We
Go From Here?*, wonderful play, very
moving about how we all had to shake
hands with the Russians and pull together
if we were to get anywhere,
on boxes,
in black drapes, wonderful what you could
do, all the boxes moved... little men
in them all the time, open stage, no tabs,
made me desperate to have a pee for them,
the whole audience rushed at the interval.
He was a lance corporal, I don't know
what happened to him,
perhaps he became a designer,
perhaps he was responsible for all that
dyed and painted hessian we wore like
silk, at least I hope I did, the
dear Motleys, the theatre in sackcloth
and ashes... hessian days.
I thought we would never be shut of it.

*Enter RODNEY unnoticed,
with sunshades. He stands behind the
chairs waiting to make his presence
with sunshades felt.
SIR GEOFFREY KENDLE continues.*

To my utter shame and constant sorrow,
consequent sorrow,
I never did do anything like my bit.

RODNEY simpers.

There was Dotty doing marvellous oil
smeared things in the water
for Korda,
and in the sand,
and over Berlin time and again...

But you don't fool anyone in this business
you know,
especially not the band,
those buggers know,
when I went to take delivery of my
knighthood the band played the Donkey
Serenade... they knew what a fraud
I was and I thought my God, had I better
dash up that carpet before the word gets
to Him?
From the kitchen?
Thank you Rodney...

*As RODNEY spreads a sunshade over
and then does the same for PENELOPE.*

... I mean if I want it, and I did
want it. I do enjoy being Sir G awfully.
I need not have worried,
apparently kings are the last to know,
queens are different and know all the
gossip,
I am glad I got Him. I used to do Him
after parties whereas I could never do
any of the girls...
Now Dotty does a terribly good Churchill,
I cannot understand why they never
use him,
as Churchill, can you?

PENELOPE: Thank you Rodney.

RODNEY: My pleasure, I nicked them from
the tables set out for the Turkish Generals.
If you're asked, you don't know.

SIR GEOFFREY KENDLE: Oh, I don't really
want it, I have got my hat,
please...

*He gets up from the chair and stands
off from it,
trying not to be associated with it.*

RODNEY: You sit down. They never do
turn up anyway!

PENELOPE: He is dull, he is old, he is
profligate...

SIR GEOFFREY KENDLE: I am sorry, have
I bored you?

PENELOPE: Not you.

SIR GEOFFREY KENDLE: Ah, Dotty!
Profligate?

PENELOPE: Yes profligate, bloody profligate.

SIR GEOFFREY KENDLE: In which sense?

PENELOPE: In every sense profligate, and I
decided this very morning to leave him.

SIR GEOFFREY KENDLE: You won't of course,
you silly girl. Where would you go? At
your age with your ankles thickening.

PENELOPE: They're not.
I shall leave him. I shall tell him I am
leaving him for you.

*SIR GEOFFREY KENDLE opening a letter,
standing off from the chairs,
angry at the presence of RODNEY who
is staring at the ground from his chin-
held position behind the chairs, one
hand holding his elbow the other across
mouth and supporting chin in the classic
camp pose, head turned away and eyes
being made to pop.*

SIR GEOFFREY KENDLE: You are not going to drag me
into it.

PENELOPE: You are dragged into it.

SIR GEOFFREY KENDLE: I am not dragged into
it Penelope. Not at all, good God I'm not
available. I thought that was well known.
Isn't it known?
It ought to be well known. Goodness me
I've had my name in the papers enough
times saying my say on the matter,
goodness me what bunkum! You should
know I'm not available...

PENELOPE: I am not convinced.

SIR GEOFFREY KENDLE: Are you not? Then be
completely convinced now that I shall not
consort with you again.
I shall certainly not marry you.

Glaring over the top of a sheet of blue
notepaper at the amused PENELOPE,
he tries to read the letter, and asks:

You're not serious?
Yes you are serious. I knew you were. I
have seen that ridiculous manner too many
times before not to know what it bodes.
When you walked into the theatre this
morning...

PENELOPE laughs.

... well it is a theatre.
Open your husband's mail and have done
with it... I've been burgled.

A sigh. He drops the hand holding
the sheet of blue notepaper to his
side,

looks at PENELOPE and RODNEY and says
again in weak despair:

I've been burgled.

PENELOPE serious and solicitous gets out
of the chair and crosses to him. He
flourishes the blue notepaper,
crumples it into a ball and tosses it
from him, not far, at his own feet in
fact.

PENELOPE: Oh Geoffrey, is it true?

SIR GEOFFREY KENDLE: Yes.

PENELOPE: Oh Geoffrey, again? How cruel.

SIR GEOFFREY KENDLE: Oh they're in and out
    'The Briars' all the time, burglars,
    they take *The Stage* and know just where I
    am at any given moment...

PENELOPE: Is *The Stage* still taken?

SIR GEOFFREY KENDLE: By burglars... Andrew
    went down.

PENELOPE: Yes, where was he when you were being
    burgled?

SIR GEOFFREY KENDLE: Lord no, I've told him
    never to be silly... Good Lord, you hear
    such dreadful things, it doesn't pay to be
    silly, he includes a list... Penelope, I just
    can't bring myself to the list,
    here, read the list Penny if you can now
    I've crumpled it...

Picking up the notepaper and trying
to smooth it out on his knee. He gives
it to PENELOPE who takes it but doesn't
attempt to read it.

... read it and please don't tell me if my
walking sticks are gone. I know they are.
Everybody knows I collect them.

RODNEY: I didn't know you collected them, I
mean, I've got one...

SIR GEOFFREY KENDLE: Look after it, it may be
valuable, and don't let a soul know you have it
or they'll covet it. I knew I was wrong to open
my mail this morning. I said as much to
you Rodney when you brought the letters
out this morning...
Why did you bring them out?

RODNEY: I'm sure.

PENELOPE: I think it's very naughty of
Andrew to tell you,
he always was a malicious old queen.

RODNEY: Speaks well of you.

PENELOPE: And you I'm sure.

RODNEY: I don't know the gentleman.

SIR GEOFFREY KENDLE: He's not malicious
darling, he's a very old and dear friend
and I suppose he thinks he is doing the
right thing letting me know.
Dumps must be distraught, poor Dumps she
must be absolutely distraught, she hates
any kind of violent upheaval. We send her
home at Christmas and get the caterers in.
They steal things.
Rodney, leave the letters at the hotel
in future,
you were never required to bring them
out, you took it upon yourself.
Can you not bear to read it?

PENELOPE: I would rather not. Anyway, I can
never read his writing.

SIR GEOFFREY KENDLE: Nobody can. I can.

He sits in his canvas chair,
dejected and near reduced to silence,
his fingers in his string bag,
he fumbles for cigarettes he
knows he hasn't got.
Says hopelessly:

You see, I know I haven't got any.
Rodney, remove this umbrella from my chair
please at once. Aren't relations with the
terrible Turks already bad enough without
you go nicking their sunshades?
I can't sit under it knowing it to be
stolen.

RODNEY: I'm ignoring him.

PENELOPE: Yes, I can see that. (*Reading the letter.*)

RODNEY: He's so bloody honest he'd rather
get sunstroke.

PENELOPE: Andrew wasn't there. (*Reading.*)

SIR GEOFFREY KENDLE: I'm so glad.
Why wasn't he there?

PENELOPE: He was up in Eaton Square.

SIR GEOFFREY KENDLE: He should have been
there. I asked him not to go to Eaton
Square, I asked him to be there with
Dumps. Who is with Dumps?

PENELOPE: Andrew is, now.

SIR GEOFFREY KENDLE: Does he say how she is?

PENELOPE: Distraught.

SIR GEOFFREY KENDLE: My very words.

PENELOPE: Are you surprised?

SIR GEOFFREY KENDLE: It does make a difference
you know. No, I can't have it, there's enough
trouble already. Please remove this umbrella.
Very well, I shall leave my chair.
I thought the Turks liked the sun in their
eyes for religious reasons,
seems a fallacy,
like us not eating fish on Fridays, I
do invariably...

He makes no move to leave the chair,
RODNEY makes no move to remove the
umbrella.
A bugle call, followed by another
and another and another, bugles
together in what would be a fanfare
if played on trumpets.

Tucket without.

RODNEY: Means they've finished, they always
have a quick joy together when they've finished.

Enter MR LAURENCE D'ORSAY murderously,
neat and tidy and murderously angry
roaring like a lion,
a sustained note. In his hand the book
dropped by the woman on her exit, the
book he stuffed into his pocket.

SIR GEOFFREY KENDLE: (*Of his entrance.*) I
don't admire the entry of the trombones!

Up out of the chair,
away from it, as MR LAURENCE D'ORSAY
goes towards it.

Don't sit there Dotty, the sunshade is
stolen property.

MR LAURENCE D'ORSAY throws the book
to the ground, rages a moment and
then sits in the chair vacated by
SIR GEOFFREY KENDLE.

RODNEY: Shall I fetch up another chair?

SIR GEOFFREY KENDLE: No, no, no, I will
not have this stealing you do Rodney. My
house has been burgled again Dotty. I have
been robbed.

PENELOPE: Good morning.

She picks up the book dropped at her
feet, opens it,
finds the envelope and reads the
address on it.

MR LAURENCE D'ORSAY: Good morning.

He looks round aggressively, at RODNEY
at GEOFFREY and then kisses PENELOPE on
her cheek, a bumping together of
jaw and teeth.

SIR GEOFFREY KENDLE: You came out of it
better than I, hardly look as if you've
crossed the road – did they stop the
battle for you? Their clapper clawing?
They seem to have stopped.
Not a sound,
was my elephant kind to you?
He's terribly sweet and kneels
down for you.
Dotty is upset, Penelope, so he won't want
to hear any of your nonsense.

PENELOPE waves the book and envelope
at her husband and asks:

PENELOPE: Is this yours, you pig? *The Wilder*
    Shores of Love?

MR LAURENCE D'ORSAY: My wife.

PENELOPE: You threw it to the ground. What
    have you done?

MR LAURENCE D'ORSAY: My beautiful young wife.

SIR GEOFFREY KENDLE: I'm sure we all think
    that, we're all terribly envious...
    Those of us who... I mean, envious, not
    in any sense me, Penelope,
    I mean I do, but I don't want you to
    think I do Penelope,
    please don't get up, I shall sit over
    here in one of these lovely chairs,
    grooves for the fingers...

MR LAURENCE D'ORSAY: Nobody is to talk
    to me, I am not to talk to anyone.

SIR GEOFFREY KENDLE: Won't, won't, why?
    Oh, the hot seat, what a hot seat.

As the chair receives him,
smiling weakly at RODNEY who smiles
back at him,
again at RODNEY who languishes another
smile,
SIR GEOFFREY then doesn't know what to
do next in this exchange of smiles,
so he looks up at the sky,
comes down again to find RODNEY still
smiling at him,
he smiles back and stands up quickly.

Too hot for me.

PENELOPE: (*Reading the envelope.*) 'The Honourable Ursula Marjoribanks'.

SIR GEOFFREY KENDLE: (*Correcting her.*) Marshbanks.

PENELOPE: Is it?

SIR GEOFFREY KENDLE: Oh yes. I don't know why I know.

PENELOPE: 'Care of the British Embassy, Ankara.'

MR LAURENCE D'ORSAY: She was just a tart to me earning her fiver a day or whatever it is.

PENELOPE: What have you done?

MR LAURENCE D'ORSAY: I am not allowed to talk.
You are not to talk to me.

PENELOPE: Geoffrey, what has he done?

SIR GEOFFREY KENDLE: Dotty, what have you done? I warn you, Penelope is about to do something conspicuously silly.

MR LAURENCE D'ORSAY waves his hand,
keeps waving it long after he has
made his point.

PENELOPE: I don't give a shit anyway.

This stops the hand from waving and
brings about silence,
she drops the book to the ground,
plonks the letters she has been
holding on to her husband's lap and
stands up,
waggles her hands behind her ears
at RODNEY and shouts:

Ears, ears.

*RODNEY shrugs and waltzes over to his
hampers,
busy bee with the plastic bags.*

Why did you not come to dinner with Bryan
last night Sir G.?
Geoffrey?

SIR GEOFFREY KENDLE: Was it a good dinner?

PENELOPE: Have you seen the boat?

SIR GEOFFREY KENDLE: I have. It bobs in the
ocean just outside my hotel room.

MR LAURENCE D'ORSAY: What does?

SIR GEOFFREY KENDLE: Bryan's boat. Is our
star able to handle it?

PENELOPE: Difficult to say, it comes complete
with captain.

SIR GEOFFREY KENDLE: Is he called today? Did
he come by boat?

PENELOPE: Have you been aboard?

SIR GEOFFREY KENDLE: No, I can't swim.

*At this MR LAURENCE D'ORSAY snorts his
contempt and rips open the large
envelope laid on his lap,
clumsy shredding of paper. He is a man
unable to do anything neatly with his
fingers.
SIR GEOFFREY talks on, but beside
himself with curiousity, edging nearer
the chairs.
Off-hand to PENELOPE:*

I'm told the one that takes you out leaks
like a sieve...

PENELOPE: It does. It sank last night.

SIR GEOFFREY KENDLE: (*Without surprise.*) Did
it? Anybody in it we know?

PENELOPE: Me.

SIR GEOFFREY KENDLE: Oh dear.

PENELOPE: And him.

SIR GEOFFREY KENDLE: Thank goodness it was
a warm night, I thought you were wet when
I met you in the corridor;
the first week we were out a thin young
girl appeared outside my window soaked to
the skin,
mouthing to be let in,
one of them,
Yale written across her chest, I'd seen
her around... did you enjoy your dinner?
I was invited. He is awfully kind Bryan,
but I couldn't face the sieve,
the land where the jumblies live,
did you have to swim?

PENELOPE: It wasn't deep. We walked.

SIR GEOFFREY KENDLE: How nice.

PENELOPE: Dotty was so pissed he started
walking the wrong way.

SIR GEOFFREY KENDLE: Did you not know
the way? It seems easy enough, I can
see it from my window,
did you get lost?

PENELOPE: We near to drowned.

SIR GEOFFREY KENDLE: That's why I wouldn't go, I wanted to.
What have you got there looks so interesting Dotty?

MR LAURENCE D'ORSAY: A script.

SIR GEOFFREY KENDLE: Oh, how nice, is it any good?
I recognize her symptoms. (*Behind his hand, whispered warning.*)

MR LAURENCE D'ORSAY: Is there any wine?

SIR GEOFFREY KENDLE: Are we all going to eat now Rodney?

RODNEY: I don't know I'm sure. Are they all coming up Mr D'Orsay?

MR LAURENCE D'ORSAY: Is there some of that Kavaklidere, is there?

RODNEY: Shall I Mrs D'Orsay?

SIR GEOFFREY KENDLE: Have you been cleared Dotty?

MR LAURENCE D'ORSAY: What?

SIR GEOFFREY KENDLE: Are you finished?

MR LAURENCE D'ORSAY: Finished? I haven't started.

SIR GEOFFREY KENDLE: Is it one of those days?

RODNEY: Only I don't think I should, do you?

PENELOPE: Don't be so boring.

SIR GEOFFREY KENDLE: One of those days when everything goes wrong,

well I won't do any more today then,
I doubt they'll get to me again if you
haven't started...
Isn't Bryan looking awful, do you think?

He stands looking off,
for a moment,
as if watching someone approach.
RODNEY looks off also.

Looks as if they're all coming up now.
He is looking dreadful.

PENELOPE: He isn't washing now that he's a
sailor. He has borrowed a yachting cap
and stopped washing. He's drinking like a
fish.

SIR GEOFFREY KENDLE: Is that to do with his
life on the ocean wave?

PENELOPE: No, not altogether. It is to do with
his marriage.

SIR GEOFFREY KENDLE: How sad, they were so
happy together. Is it over?

PENELOPE: It may well be.

SIR GEOFFREY KENDLE: Have I met her?

MR LAURENCE D'ORSAY flicking through
the pages of the script,
SIR GEOFFREY KENDLE goes to look over
his shoulder and then says suddenly:

He isn't married!

PENELOPE: No.

SIR GEOFFREY KENDLE: I knew.

PENELOPE: He had made arrangements to be.

SIR GEOFFREY KENDLE: Now that is something
   I never did. At least not with the people
   I actually came to marry.

PENELOPE: It was to be in the Blue Mosque.

SIR GEOFFREY KENDLE: Oh wonderful, that
   would have been nice. Have you seen the
   Blue Mosque, Dotty?

PENELOPE: Yes, we all went. Remember?

SIR GEOFFREY KENDLE: I do. That's right,
   quite wonderful. Smells of feet.

PENELOPE: Smells of feet.

   They say it together. PENELOPE giggles.

MR LAURENCE D'ORSAY: What are you giggling
   at?

PENELOPE: The Blue Mosque.

MR LAURENCE D'ORSAY: Are you.

   *He says sourly, putting the script
   behind him. SIR GEOFFREY KENDLE
   asks him:*

SIR GEOFFREY KENDLE: Anything interesting?

   *MR LAURENCE D' ORSAY ignores him,
   SIR GEOFFREY KENDLE redirects his
   attention to the coming of BRYAN.
   Looking off and saying:*

   Would Bryan not have to become a Mussulman?

PENELOPE: Not if he marries a Mussulman.

SIR GEOFFREY KENDLE: He wouldn't be so
   unkind, they wear those baggy trousers!

How very naughty of him,
where did you hear this,
she's not... surely she's not a... ?

PENELOPE: I was there. I overheard them making
tentative inquiry as to the possibility of
a white wedding in the Blue Mosque,
true,
chatting up the local dervish,
albeit concomitant with his concurrent
coalescence of world-wide movie commitment.

SIR GEOFFREY KENDLE: He's not American.

PENELOPE: Not yet, but circumcision is not
far off, I feel he will be admitted,
he has the words,
he has the faith,
he has the urges,
he has the world-wide commitments...

SIR GEOFFREY KENDLE: He's got a London voice.
That whine they all have,
you all have it, he could come from anywhere
but over there...

PENELOPE: She is.
You know her. You've met her.

SIR GEOFFREY KENDLE: I expect so if she's one
of the Americans, I meet all the Americans.
They seem to like me.
Oh well, we don't have to be involved and
go through all that dishonesty,
I mean if it's not anyone we know and love,
I mean we won't have to go or anything,
I mean you can't be rude to Americans,
they don't believe it,
I mean I can't be, they're too busy liking
the way you talk I find, with me...

PENELOPE: Anyway, it's off now.

RODNEY: Do I give the mister some wine?

> *Standing close to PENELOPE, a bottle of*
> *white wine dripping moisture,*
> *a plastic cup,*
> *RODNEY asks with lowered voice and*
> *a great deal of concerned eye rolling*
> *in the direction of D'ORSAY;*
> *SIR GEOFFREY smiles on the bottle.*

SIR GEOFFREY KENDLE: Aaaaaaah!

RODNEY: You don't usually Sir G, when
    you're working,
    he goes to sleep you see if he drinks
    in the middle of the day, does sir,
    which is why I don't push the *sarap*
    when his tongue is hanging out,
    the *sarap* love, wine,
    do I give it to hubby?

SIR GEOFFREY KENDLE: Thank you Rodney.

RODNEY: Well, if you're sure you're
    not going to be called this afternoon,
    I should hate you to be dozy,
    I mean I shall get the blame in all
    the subsequent books,
    like poor Miss Thing with Ivor...
    Here he is then,
    Errol Flynn's fife and drum.

> *Looking off, anticipating*
> *the entrance of BRYAN DAVID,*
> *a nod and whisper to PENELOPE.*

Elbow the *sarap* with hubby then?

PENELOPE: Go away.

RODNEY: I'm sure.

*Enter BRYAN DAVID, slight, a lot of
black hair and a moustache which is
very frail and requires constant
tugging. He is dressed in costume
cavalry overalls,
a T-shirt with Yale written across
it, a sword and a swordbelt,
Turkish cavalry boots.*

BRYAN DAVID: Do you like the boots?

PENELOPE: Good morning.

BRYAN DAVID: Good morning Sir Geoffrey, what a
place eh?

SIR GEOFFREY KENDLE: Isn't it, I feel
awful Bryan but might I cadge some fags,
congratulations by the way,
I hope you'll both be very happy,
have you got any? I came out without
and I've been cadging ever since.

BRYAN DAVID: That's how I got these boots,
my groom,
aren't they great, he'll get stick.

SIR GEOFFREY KENDLE: Thank you Rodney.

*RODNEY has thrust out a cigarette
with a great deal of reproach in his
manner.
SIR GEOFFREY KENDLE takes it regretfully.
RODNEY whispers:*

RODNEY: Why don't you ask me?

SIR GEOFFREY KENDLE: It's terribly kind of
you Rodney, but I don't like to keep bumming

from you,
oh dear, you know what I mean... did you
come by boat Bryan?

PENELOPE: Little difficult cherub, no water.

SIR GEOFFREY KENDLE: Is there not?
I haven't looked. I thought I read somewhere
there was water...

*Going over to his chair to look for
his guide book, MR LAURENCE D'ORSAY
glaring at him as
he approaches,
SIR GEOFFREY KENDLE not very brave,
gives up,
holding the bottle and plastic cup,
offers it to MR LAURENCE D'ORSAY
who takes it,
SIR GEOFFREY still talking, the unlit
cigarette bobbing in his teeth
as he does so.*

... that Priene was a port of some sort,
had a harbour,
it's in my bag when I can get it,
I'm sure...

BRYAN DAVID: Ah you see, it used to be.

PENELOPE: Why are you wearing that sword?

BRYAN DAVID: Good morning Penny.

PENELOPE: You weren't called this morning
were you?

BRYAN DAVID: I thought I might school my horse
a little, it's all you this morning Sir
Geoffrey, isn't it?
That marvellous speech.

SIR GEOFFREY KENDLE: Thank you, I hope I
do it justice.

MR LAURENCE D'ORSAY: You always do.

PENELOPE: Yes, he always does.

SIR GEOFFREY KENDLE: What it is to have
friends.

> *BRYAN DAVID has mounted the seats of*
> *the amphitheatre two at a stride and*
> *stands some way up,*
> *a booted pose. They all wait for the*
> *inevitable arm flung out,*
> *he flings it. SIR GEOFFREY KENDLE*
> *hopes to sit down, has moved to be in*
> *a position to sink wearily into his*
> *chair. PENELOPE gazes up at BRYAN with*
> *mock intense interest.*
> *He says, pointing:*

BRYAN DAVID: That stretch of flat land you can
see is the Plain of the Meander.

SIR GEOFFREY KENDLE: Is it?
Is he talking to me? I beg your pardon
Bryan, you're so splendid up there,
isn't he splendid? A young Douglas.

BRYAN DAVID: Join me. Come here.

PENELOPE: Bryan, do you need to wear that
sword all the time?

BRYAN DAVID: I'm getting my horse used to it.

PENELOPE: Should you not be sitting on him,
to get him used to it?
Is he not a cavalry horse and used to it?

BRYAN DAVID: No darling, he is a very expensive
mare brought from England.

SIR GEOFFREY KENDLE: Dotty, you're sitting in
    my chair.

MR LAURENCE D'ORSAY: Then you sit in mine.

BRYAN DAVID: You see there was water right across
    to Miletus. Have you seen Miletus, Sir G.?

SIR GEOFFREY KENDLE: No. Is it absolutely
    marvellous?
    Dotty, I would rather sit in my own chair
    if you don't mind, it does have my name
    rather nicely painted on the back.

MR LAURENCE D'ORSAY: I'm settled.

BRYAN DAVID: Do you know anything about Greek
    theatres Sir Geoffrey?

PENELOPE: Everything.

BRYAN DAVID: Does he?

PENELOPE: He says he does, very wearily. I
    think it means he never wants to play
    Oedipus again...

BRYAN DAVID: Have you seen Miletus, Penny?

PENELOPE: No. Dotty will never go anywhere. I
    want to go to Ephesus.

BRYAN DAVID: You can just see it. Miletus.

She climbs up the stepped seats,
BRYAN coming some way down for her,
putting out a hand for her,
she stops and shades her eyes to look out
over the Plain of the Meander.

PENELOPE: Where is it?

BRYAN DAVID: You should be able to.

He climbs up some more, and PENELOPE
follows. RODNEY shouts after them,
his hands on his hips,
hot and annoyed, wiping his forehead
with the back of his arm.

RODNEY: You're not going up the hill? I've
got yours down here.
They're going up,
you'll have to come down, it's liver and
bacon up the hill, she won't like that.

BRYAN and PENELOPE are climbing out of
sight, displacing earth and small
stones as they scramble upwards.
A laugh as one of them slithers and
a tiny avalanche threatens those
below. SIR GEOFFREY might follow but is
put off by the fall of earth. He suggests
instead to DOTTY,
indicating the empty chair.

SIR GEOFFREY KENDLE: You see, you will want
to give your chair to Penny.

MR LAURENCE D'ORSAY: She can have my chair.
I thought that was my chair. Isn't that my
chair? Yes it is, it's got my name painted
on the back.

SIR GEOFFREY KENDLE: Dotty, you're sitting
on my things. Don't be unpleasant, it does
not become you.

MR LAURENCE D'ORSAY: (*Quite serious and urgent.*)
Geoffrey, will you let me talk to you?
They have sent me off the set, nobody is
to talk to me and I am not to talk to
anyone, there is talk of sending me home

and dropping me from the picture.
My God I was fucking angry. You saw?
Sent off the set in front of the entire
cast...

SIR GEOFFREY KENDLE: It's mostly elephant
and horse today Dotty...

MR LAURENCE D'ORSAY: Geoffrey, I can't be sent
off another film.

SIR GEOFFREY KENDLE: Are there any more
chairs Rodney?

RODNEY: Have you not got a chair?

SIR GEOFFREY KENDLE: I'm thinking of Penny.
Mrs D'Orsay.

RODNEY: Has she not got a chair?

Exit RODNEY, busy.

MR LAURENCE D'ORSAY: Geoffrey, will you
talk to him? I can't talk to them without
wanting to knock seven colours of shit out
of them...

SIR GEOFFREY KENDLE: I mean, surely he won't
drop you from the picture...

MR LAURENCE D'ORSAY: He will.

SIR GEOFFREY KENDLE: But Dotty you thrive
on being dropped from pictures,
and when you go to see them you're delighted.

MR LAURENCE D'ORSAY: I know about this one.
This is the one that means I'll never work
again, for anyone.

SIR GEOFFREY KENDLE: But you shouldn't
work again for anyone, you're quite awful,
and you've been hitting Penelope.

MR LAURENCE D'ORSAY: Very well, up you
    Sir Geoffrey.

SIR GEOFFREY KENDLE: You've said that before.
    Much more colourfully. What have you done
    this time?

MR LAURENCE D'ORSAY: The usual thing, I mean...
    the usual thing, that woman complained.
    You'd think she'd never seen one before. It
    seems she is the daughter of the British
    Ambassador.

SIR GEOFFREY KENDLE: Does it seem that?

MR LAURENCE D'ORSAY: Yes. I thought she
    was just some Turkish extra you see,
    they very rarely complain; the
    brazen bitch!

SIR GEOFFREY KENDLE: You must apologize.

MR LAURENCE D'ORSAY: I did. I went down
    on my knees.

SIR GEOFFREY KENDLE: Yes, you would.

MR LAURENCE D'ORSAY: You must say that you
    can't work without me.

SIR GEOFFREY KENDLE: I suppose so.

MR LAURENCE D'ORSAY: Will you?

SIR GEOFFREY KENDLE: I suppose so.

*Enter PENELOPE at a run down the stone
stairs, followed by BRYAN.*

PENELOPE: You can't see Miletus.

BRYAN DAVID: You can see where it is.
    Do you know anything about Greek theatres
    Sir Geoffrey?

SIR GEOFFREY KENDLE: You've asked me that
    before. Do you mean this Greek theatre or
    the state of the theatre in Athens?

BRYAN DAVID: Is that an eagle?

SIR GEOFFREY KENDLE: We decided.

PENELOPE: We saw it earlier.

SIR GEOFFREY KENDLE: It's always been there.

PENELOPE: If they have them in Turkey.

BRYAN DAVID: They do. Why not?

SIR GEOFFREY KENDLE: He'll know. I said
    ask Bryan because he'll be sure to know.

PENELOPE: Get out of Geoffrey's chair Dotty.

MR LAURENCE D'ORSAY: Are you talking to me?

SIR GEOFFREY KENDLE: Are you surprised? You
    should be.

PENELOPE: Sit in your own chair.

SIR GEOFFREY KENDLE: It's all right, it's
    all right really, it's just that the ground
    is so hard and hot.

BRYAN DAVID: I won't have this nonsense of names
    on chairs. I don't have a chair.

SIR GEOFFREY KENDLE: Good for you. It's awfully
    silly I know but it's the only
    way you can be sure of somewhere to sit.
    I never sit in anyone else's chair.

PENELOPE: He has got a chair.

BRYAN DAVID: I have not.

PENELOPE: You have. It's always put there
for you and it's the only one without a
name on it,
everybody knows it's your chair and they
are careful not to sit on it. I always
sit on the chair with the grandest name.

BRYAN DAVID: How else?

PENELOPE: How else what?

BRYAN DAVID: How else do you get to meet the
grandest people?

PENELOPE: Try living with them.

BRYAN DAVID: I had a chair on my first film. I
got sick of the birds sitting in it.
Plastic cups. (*He notices.*)

SIR GEOFFREY KENDLE: (*Sorrowfully.*) Yes,
they'll never rot or anything.

BRYAN DAVID: I went for a long ride this morning
miles and far from anyone and anything to
do with us,
not a sign of a plastic cup anywhere,
actually I began to worry a little because
I thought I might well be lost.
Who said no such luck?

SIR GEOFFREY KENDLE: Nobody said that.

PENELOPE: What would we do for a star if you
got lost?

BRYAN DAVID: Find another.

PENELOPE: How very practical of you.

MR LAURENCE D'ORSAY: Don't imagine it would
be impossible.

BRYAN DAVID: I don't.

SIR GEOFFREY KENDLE: Find me a curled young man.

MR LAURENCE D'ORSAY: That has never been difficult.

BRYAN DAVID: I did say, find another...

SIR GEOFFREY KENDLE: A more curled young man.

MR LAURENCE D'ORSAY: Good God, you're two a penny.

BRYAN DAVID: I rather think I said that, Dotty.

MR LAURENCE D'ORSAY: Your modesty doesn't hold water mate.

SIR GEOFFREY KENDLE: Like his boat.

BRYAN DAVID: I'm sorry about that, it went down with all hands.

SIR GEOFFREY KENDLE: So I hear.

MR LAURENCE D'ORSAY: You wouldn't have got me into it...

PENELOPE: You were in it.

SIR GEOFFREY KENDLE: Were you not in it? No wonder you got wet...

MR LAURENCE D'ORSAY: If I had known.

PENELOPE: You were so fucking pissed you wouldn't have known if it had a hole in it the size of a manhole...

SIR GEOFFREY KENDLE: (*Aside to BRYAN.*) Oh thank goodness, they're now going to get it off their chests.

BRYAN DAVID: Is it my fault?

SIR GEOFFREY KENDLE: Oh please, it's the
    best thing that could happen... and no
    way your fault at all.

*He states hopefully, standing well off
from PENELOPE and DOTTY,
steering BRYAN by his elbow towards
the food laid out by RODNEY.
RODNEY flapping his hand over the
food spread on the ground and tearing
bread at the same time.*

RODNEY: It's liver and bacon for them
    up the hill but I knew you wouldn't touch
    it. Can I leave you now?
    Have you got all you want do you think,
    there's your salt look,
    will you want anything else?

*SIR GEOFFREY KENDLE is waiting for
the expected outburst from PENELOPE
and MR LAURENCE D'ORSAY,
it doesn't come. D'ORSAY glowers at his wife
for a moment and then looks away
in some embarrassment.*

BRYAN DAVID: I was saying I rode for miles and
    thought you were all left behind.

SIR GEOFFREY KENDLE: How wonderful. I
    got in a car and went to Antalya the
    other day,
    exhausting,
    an obscene petrified waterfall on the way,
    quite marvellous; they sent a telegram
    ordering me back.
    Luckily I got it.

BRYAN DAVID: I looked down on the ground and
    thought they were stones my horse was picking

here way through very carefully,
but they were moving. Tortoises.

SIR GEOFFREY KENDLE: They won't stand on them
will they?

RODNEY: I shall be back as soon as I've
seen to them up the hill,
you let me know if there's anything you
want...

*Rubbing his hands and twirling on his
toes, he takes a white apron from
inside his shirt,
shakes it and wraps it round his waist,
tying it at the back as he backs away.*

Only I'm on now.

BRYAN DAVID: Aeschylus had a tortoise dropped
in his head by an eagle couldn't open the
can, mistook his bald head for a handy
white stone.

RODNEY: Ooooooh!

SIR GEOFFREY KENDLE: Why I always wear a
hat.

RODNEY: Are you coming up Bryan David?

BRYAN DAVID: Yes.

SIR GEOFFREY KENDLE: Do stay.

BRYAN DAVID: I'm playing cards.

SIR GEOFFREY KENDLE: Aaaah! I'm sure there's
plenty of wine...

BRYAN DAVID: See you later.

RODNEY: If you're coming up.

RODNEY backing up the hill formed by the
stone seats of the small amphitheatre,
opening his arms in the 'love you and leave
you' manner to the glowering MR LAURENCE
D'ORSAY and disconsolate SIR GEOFFREY KENDLE.
Exit BRYAN up the hill.

SIR GEOFFREY KENDLE: It's chairs really
Rodney, can you not find another one for
us, up the hill?

RODNEY: They'll all be took Sir G.
You are silly not sitting in that
one. Hitler is sitting in yours, you sit
in Hitler's.

SIR GEOFFREY KENDLE: Mr D'Orsay has given
his chair to his wife you see, he has a
perfect right...

RODNEY flounces back down the stone
seats and pulls the sunshades from
the chairs, very quickly and expertly
they come down;
tucked, one under each arm and swinging
dangerously lengthily over the ducked
head of MR LAURENCE D'ORSAY as he reaches
for his straw hat under the chair next
to him. Not pausing in movement, RODNEY
whips the canvas backs from the chairs
and changes the names on the chairs as
MR LAURENCE D'ORSAY is about to lean
back, having acquired his hat;
RODNEY then puts the final touch by
lifting SIR GEOFFREY's string bag from
one chair to the other,
fastidiously; camp and swift the whole
business, his heels spurting little
puffs of applause as he exits with a

*last pitying look and smile at SIR
GEOFFREY over his shoulder from row ten,
before he exits.
Exit RODNEY up the hill.*

...oh, thank you Rodney, thank you.

*SIR GEOFFREY sinks gratefully into the
chair now bearing his name,
lifts his hat from his head and wafts
air around his face; replaces the hat
on his head. He looks for his letters,
tugs at the large package addressed to
him which is being sat on by D'ORSAY.
MR LAURENCE D'ORSAY eases himself in
his seat to allow the package to be
pulled from under him,
staring straight ahead, the bottle of
wine and plastic cup held in his hands
before him. SIR GEOFFREY KENDLE slits
open the package neatly and swiftly
with his thumb-nail and is about to
take out the script enclosed when he
notices that MR LAURENCE D'ORSAY is
shaking his large head slowly from
side to side, a painful and lugubrious
movement, very sad, like the inexorable
swing peculiar to elephants and every
bit as pitiable.
SIR GEOFFREY KENDLE casts his face
into a suitably soft expression; he
does after all dote on elephants,
begins to swing his own head almost in
time and on the upswing notices PENELOPE
still there, looking at her husband and
hating him.*

Darling, darling, there you are, we were
doing elephants.

Leaping to his feet.

I thought you were gone off with our star,
Penelope, please have my chair.

*Regretfully he indicates the chair and
is delighted at her reply.*

PENELOPE: No. No thanks Geoffrey, it's all
   right. I'm going to look at my Benjyhorse.
   Not that I'm dressed for riding.
   Why don't you come?

SIR GEOFFREY KENDLE: Difficult darling.
   I like it known where I am and I said
   I would be here,
   it does save those boys such trouble,
   those white-faced second assistants
   with their burned-off noses,
   how they can be so sunburned and yet so
   pale and exhausted... do you know I got
   my call sheet at midnight last night?
   and they were still doing the rounds,
   couldn't find Dotty.
   I like them to be sure they know where
   to find me,
   one wouldn't want to be responsible for
   them ranging the hills on their sticks
   of legs... I said I would be here you
   see.

PENELOPE: Geoffrey, you make them sound
   like *gamins grillés*... or something,
   gamins en croute?

SIR GEOFFREY KENDLE: Dotty ought to have
   you if you can bear it, he is beginning
   to moon,
   might well be blubbing under that hat.

PENELOPE: Like underpriviledged East Enders
    desperately tramping the Margate sands
    for a bit of spare before the coach
    takes off...

SIR GEOFFREY KENDLE: I do know he is
    furiously upset for the fear he has
    entirely burned his boats this time,
    the Embassy involved...
    Poor Dotty, I hate to be left alone with
    him in this state.
    Poor Dotty?

*He asks hopefully of PENELOPE who smiles
at her husband for a moment of silence
and then says as she leaves:*

PENELOPE: Yes.

*Exit PENELOPE with SIR GEOFFREY KENDLE
calling after her, concerned.*

SIR GEOFFREY KENDLE: Penelope I do entreat
    you not to traipse through the stables
    dressed as you are,
    I think you should wear something.
    Dotty, should you not go with her? Is it
    wise she should go alone to the stables?
    She's got very little on,
    very beautiful but very little, you can
    see all her hairs! Who dresses her?
    You see she's chosen badly,
    the material catches on them,
    very beautiful but one is bound to notice
    and stare,
    they ruck up her tuck most distractingly,
    should she not wear silk which is heavier? If
    she is set on fashionably dispensing with
    knickers, very beautiful but you see with

all the will in the world you can't
stand there talking about polite things
with your eyes fixed,
as they are, as they are drawn... even I
find it impossible to have a serious
conversation with her when she's dressed
so alarmingly... should you not go?
Dotty, you understand these terms, what
does 'Hair in the gate' mean?

He tries, left alone with the gently
swinging head of MR LAURENCE D'ORSAY
and beginning to clutch at straws.

Is it a compliment? They call it out
after all my scenes, *encore*?

To his horror, the head stops its
swinging, SIR GEOFFREY KENDLE casts
around for sanctuary. MR LAURENCE D'ORSAY
lifts his grief-stricken face to utter
and SIR GEOFFREY comes in quickly:.

All right Dotty, I'll see what I can do for
you, you bugger, all right I'll talk to our
director for you, see what can be done,
the Embassy involved.

Indecision, with the package/envelope
in his hand he starts to leave, then comes
back to get his things. D'ORSAY has
his arm over the back of the chair,
a hand on the seat of the chair next
to him.
SIR GEOFFREY KENDLE puts out a
hand to tug his string bag clear.

I don't know how long I'll be. You see
Trevor is very busy shooting.

MR LAURENCE D'ORSAY: Do you get me out
of this one Geoffrey I'll thank you.

SIR GEOFFREY KENDLE: I wanted to take
some pictures... but never mind.

MR LAURENCE D'ORSAY: Leave them with me,
I'll look after your things for you.

SIR GEOFFREY KENDLE: Is it not a dreadful
bore should you want to wander off? are
you sure you don't want to ride with
Penelope, my goodness she wouldn't! Look
I'll happily stay and look after things,
my things,
and see Trevor later,
if you want to go off, patch things up
with Penny, stop her from doing something
sorry!

MR LAURENCE D'ORSAY: The least I can do.

SIR GEOFFREY KENDLE: Are you sure?
Well, if it's no trouble. Things are
stolen so easily,
and I put a new roll of film in the
Brownie this morning, I'd hate to lose it,
I've got to use it quickly because
the camera seeps in light over a period
of time... very well.

Enter RODNEY down the hill.
Exit SIR GEOFFREY up the hill saying:

Thank you.

*And to RODNEY as he passes him on
the stone seats:*

Rodney, hush, but can you get me a chair
up there, I'm exhausted?

*Exit SIR GEOFFREY KENDLE with RODNEY's
assurance. Leaving MR LAURENCE D'ORSAY
to close his eyes and tip back in his
chair so that it is balanced on its
rear legs, the bottle of wine held
between his legs.
RODNEY at the ice box pulls out a
dripping bottle,
wipes it on his apron, wipes his own
sweat-wet face on the cold wet cloth
and contemplates MR LAURENCE D'ORSAY.
In a mixture of admiration and affection
for a rogue he says quietly a whisper:*

RODNEY: Drunken old sod.

And then a little louder:

I say, you'll fall off of that chair and
crack your starting handle if you don't
take care... drunken old sod,
still whipping it out and placing it in
their hands at your age!
Mind you I could go mad myself,
without I had self-control, what with
grown young men holding hands and
walking like gazelles... still.
Talk to yourself Rodney.

*Suddenly, his face red and his eyes
tight shut RODNEY shrieks:*

Are you listening, are you listening,
are you listening to me Mr Laurence?

*Startled, MR LAURENCE D'ORSAY opens
his eyes and says quite truthfully:*

MR LAURENCE D'ORSAY: Well, no. I'm not.

RODNEY: I know you're not, I know.

MR LAURENCE D'ORSAY: Should I be?

RODNEY: I would be grateful, it would be
nice. We are all out here on an artistic
venture.

*This pronouncement greeted by MR
LAURENCE D'ORSAY in astonished eyes
popping silence. RODNEY tries to add
a little more forcefully:*

I mean, fuck me, aren't we?
Flasher?

*Cradling the bottle and pulling out
another RODNEY starts up the hill,
stopping on the way to peer pointedly
over MR LAURENCE D'ORSAY's shoulder,
at the bottle still held by the actor
between his legs, commenting:*

I see you're using a stand-in!

*Exit RODNEY with this parting shot,
up the hill. A bottle in each hand,
he uses them to thrust and balance
as he scales the crumbling seats of
the amphitheatre.
MR LAURENCE D'ORSAY finds himself solus.
The curtain comes down.*

ACT TWO

Scene 1

A hill overlooking the amphitheatre.

The curtain rises.
Dazzling white plywood reflectors in
a shape almost triangular, the base
downstage and the blunt apex jutted
under a high scaffold tower. The
reflectors face out. Above them and
forming a ceiling banners of white
muslin are stretched to filter the
sun. On the tower rickety planks form
platforms at various levels reached
by ladders and ropes. At the highest
point of the tower there is assumed to
be a camera, but the top of the tower
is out of sight. Powerful lights are
swung up into the tower, clamped to
the framework, cables loop and drop
drumming to the ground. Two 'brutes'
are set to peer over the top edge of two of
the largest reflectors. None of
the lights are switched on.
There are gaps between the plywood
frames but they mask completely. The
result is intense white glare.
Enter SIR GEOFFREY KENDLE; a look of
concentration. A slow studied stride to a point
in the centre of the stage formed by the intimidating
whiteness. A shout through
a megaphone from above: 'Stop!'
He stops and stands still, raising his
head to look up into the sky.

Out of the glare a grotesque;
naked but for the smallest pair of
khaki shorts, BERNIE THE VOLT.
BERNIE is a very fat and very red
cockney electrician. He has an enormous
stomach emphasized by his low slung
shorts and leather belt. He wears gloves
of asbestos, yellow short socks and
suede shoes, a silver paper nose-shield
held to his face by camera tape and the
tools of his trade in his leather belt;
a black rubber-handled hammer,
a pair of insulated pliers,
a long screwdriver,
inserted in a pouch to dangle between
his legs, the length used by BERNIE
for every inch of its comic phallic
value. He glistens with grease and
keeps his face averted when in the
presence of theatrical knights. He
shouts as he enters:

BERNIE: No, it's all right mate, no. No
fucking shop stewards watching is there?

At the feet of SIR GEOFFREY he sprawls,
a piece of two inch batten in his hand;
he whips out his black hammer and pins
it to the ground with two swift strokes,
before SIR GEOFFREY can recoil,
the batten tight against SIR GEOFFREY's
toes, BERNIE grinning up at him.

You don't mind my language guv'nor,
too bleeding bad if you do... on
your marks, get set.

Exit BERNIE THE VOLT backwards shamble
into the white glare, inserting his

hammer into its pouch, grinning into
space a few inches to the left of SIR
GEOFFREY's eyes. His hair is a shock
of pure white.
Leaving SIR GEOFFREY KENDLE standing
alone, his feet wedged tight by the
batten. He stands still for a long
time and then answers a remark
by megaphone from on high.

SIR GEOFFREY KENDLE: No, no, really, really
I don't mind, you just get it right please.

Another remark by megaphone from the sky.

I'm glad I came up,
I thought you were all at lunch, I didn't
know disaster had struck yet again,
what was it,
there was some talk of liver and bacon?

More megaphone and
a braying laugh gratifies SIR GEOFFREY;
he laughs and answers:

No thank you, I'm not hungry in this heat,
well yes I would like a drink of some
sort, I was about to have a drink...

Enter a can of Buddweiser beer, from on high
in the hand of TREVOR HOLLINGSHEAD.
Enter TREVOR HOLLINGSHEAD who has skin
the brightest shade of burned red,
his face scuffed with skin from previous
burnings and daubed with white cream,
a large blob melting on his nose.
He is tall and thin and utterly happy.
He wears a yellow orange checked flannel shirt,
white denim trousers, white plimsolls,
white socks and a white silk windcheater

with red, blue and white striped collar,
cuffs and waist. He carries a chattering radio transceiver.
He approaches SIR GEOFFREY beer can
first, his other hand pushing back
his hair nervously again and again,
grinning, still a part of the reflectors, the tower,
still attuned to chatter, to which he
constantly answers and asks 'What?'
He opens the can of beer, gives it
to SIR GEOFFREY.

SIR GEOFFREY KENDLE: Thank you Trevor.

TREVOR HOLLINGSHEAD: What?

SIR GEOFFREY KENDLE: Cold!

TREVOR HOLLINGSHEAD: Do you want a cup?

SIR GEOFFREY KENDLE: No, no, it's so cold.

TREVOR HOLLINGSHEAD: Here, hold it to your
brow, isn't that super?

He pushes the can in SIR GEOFFREY's
hand up to SIR GEOFFREY's brow and holds it there.

SIR GEOFFREY KENDLE: Marvellous, marvellous,
might I drink some?

TREVOR HOLLINGSHEAD: Please do. You don't want
a cup or anything?

SIR GEOFFREY KENDLE: No please, fine.
It's so marvellous to get some real beer.
Isn't it?

TREVOR HOLLINGSHEAD: Can't you get any?

SIR GEOFFREY KENDLE: I don't drink it.

TREVOR HOLLINGSHEAD: I'm sorry, what
would you like? Would you like some Dom
Perignon, Geoffrey?

SIR GEOFFREY KENDLE: No no, this is
    marvellous... I mean so much better
    than the Turkish beer.
    I mean, and I do mean this... thank
    you.

    And he drinks the beer as quickly as
    he can before he can say anything else.
    TREVOR HOLLINGSHEAD laughs and claps
    his hands in delight, laughs again,
    rubs his hands and says softly to
    himself: 'Super', then:

    Have you tasted Turkish champagne?

TREVOR HOLLINGSHEAD: No I haven't, is it
    marvellous?

SIR GEOFFREY KENDLE: No.

TREVOR HOLLINGSHEAD: Don't you like the wine?

SIR GEOFFREY KENDLE: The white wine, splendid.

TREVOR HOLLINGSHEAD: Yes, isn't it, I mean it's
    nice, super.
    What? (*Into radio.*)

SIR GEOFFREY KENDLE: Yes.

TREVOR HOLLINGSHEAD: Sorry, can you walk back
    on to your mark? Sorry Geoffrey.

SIR GEOFFREY KENDLE: No, please.

TREVOR HOLLINGSHEAD: What?

    TREVOR HOLLINGSHEAD listening,
    looking up at where the camera is
    assumed to be, his head cocked, his
    hand holding SIR GEOFFREY KENDLE at
    elbow, steering him, saying:

Yes, super, all right super.
Geoffrey, they want you to go back and
walk on to your mark once more, please.
They're so incompetent! What?

He shouts into the radio, to hoots
of laughter, to BERNIE poking his head
round, his braying 'what' and little boy
grin directed at SIR GEOFFREY KENDLE
who tut-tuts.

Aren't they Geoffrey?

SIR GEOFFREY KENDLE: Oh dear no. Never let
it be said.

TREVOR HOLLINGSHEAD: Say louder you think
they're incompetent, Geoffrey. Sir Geoffrey
wants his lunch. (*Offering radio.*)

SIR GEOFFREY KENDLE: Oh no, please, my future
is after all in their hands, they might well
decide to make me look a fool... I am as it
were, in their hands...

He raises his arms in mock surrender,
his hands palm out.
TREVOR laughs and shaking his head
says seriously,
but following quickly with another hoot
of laughter:

TREVOR HOLLINGSHEAD: *My* hands.

That shy laugh and backing step,
grinning, rubbing, backing off from
SIR GEOFFREY KENDLE who smiles and
raises his hands again, not quite
so much as before,
backing away himself to a point near
to one of the reflectors:

SIR GEOFFREY KENDLE: *Your*hands.
    Is this far enough back? I shall ask for
    more money I think, I almost never do. I
    hear the Turks want more money?

TREVOR HOLLINGSHEAD: That's far enough
    back Sir Geoffrey. Is that far enough back?
    What? No listen, forget your own nonsense,
    I've got a very important actor down here
    who doesn't have to put up with any of
    your nonsense. Is that far enough back?
    Stay there.
    It depends on how far back I want you. Do
    I have to climb up that fucking tower again?
    Yes. Are you all right Geoffrey for a
    moment while I have a look?

SIR GEOFFREY KENDLE: Please, please do.

TREVOR HOLLINGSHEAD: What?

SIR GEOFFREY KENDLE: I said please...

    But TREVOR HOLLINGSHEAD is listening
    to his cameraman, his ear to the radio. He says into it:

TREVOR HOLLINGSHEAD: No, I don't want to. I
    want to stay down here and rehearse Sir G.,
    I've got an actor standing around here
    waiting on you. All right.

    He comes over to SIR GEOFFREY KENDLE
    still nodding and talking, listening,
    holding the actor, walking, holding him
    by the elbow,
    and listening to the chatter he can hear
    from the radio. He grins.

    You ought to sit down, this is going to
    take an age. Would you like your chair
    brought?

SIR GEOFFREY KENDLE: Would that be an
awful lot of trouble?

TREVOR HOLLINGSHEAD: Doesn't matter if it
is, you are to cause trouble if you want to.

SIR GEOFFREY KENDLE: Only if it's no trouble.

TREVOR HOLLINGSHEAD: Bernie, get out of that
fucking chair and give it to Sir Geoffrey.
Here.
Not there, here.

*Enter BERNIE THE VOLT with chair,
which he places for SIR GEOFFREY at
a point indicated by TREVOR's finger.*

SIR GEOFFREY KENDLE: Thank you Bernie.

TREVOR HOLLINGSHEAD: I shall stand here
for you. You can get me another can of
beer. (*To BERNIE.*)

SIR GEOFFREY KENDLE: Would you like some of this?

TREVOR HOLLINGSHEAD: No. They can get me
another.

*Exit BERNIE with TREVOR HOLLINGSHEAD
calling after him.*

Give them all some beer Bernie.

SIR GEOFFREY KENDLE: Ah!

TREVOR HOLLINGSHEAD: What?

*TREVOR asks of SIR GEOFFREY, cocking
his head and grinning, shy, hoping
that SIR GEOFFREY's interjection was
one of approval, asks again:*

What?

SIR GEOFFREY KENDLE: I think I said something like 'ah'. Not important.

TREVOR HOLLINGSHEAD: What?

Rubbing his hands, running on the spot, slapping the top of his legs, TREVOR HOLLINGSHEAD refuses to believe that SIR GEOFFREY is not impressed by his generosity towards his camera crew.

Give all those greedy buggers some beer.

SIR GEOFFREY KENDLE sits down and asks:

SIR GEOFFREY KENDLE: Do I not have my terrible Turkish stand- in today Trevor, I mean do you have to... ?

TREVOR HOLLINGSHEAD: I am your stand-in today, Geoffrey.

SIR GEOFFREY KENDLE: My word, I am honoured.

TREVOR HOLLINGSHEAD: It's only because I'm cheap. What?
They say it's only because I'm cheap.

SIR GEOFFREY KENDLE: Yes.
I hear the terrible Turks are asking for more money, all of them?

TREVOR HOLLINGSHEAD: I'm not cheap.

SIR GEOFFREY KENDLE: No no. I fear that I am not cheap.

TREVOR HOLLINGSHEAD: You are quite cheap.

SIR GEOFFREY KENDLE continues for a moment without considering this very seriously delivered statement.

SIR GEOFFREY KENDLE: I know I'm awfully
   silly about... am I?

TREVOR HOLLINGSHEAD: Yes you are.

SIR GEOFFREY KENDLE: I'm not a bit surprised.

*But he is, and taken aback he takes
refuge in confusion and humorous self-
deprecation as is invariable with him.*

I knew there must be some good reason for
my being constantly employed.
I knew. I never know. People always lie
don't they? About money? Say one thing to
the papers and another in private? Not that
I ever ask anybody what salary they're on.
When I have actually been asked to produce
a play on the stage or something I've found
out of course and been amazed!
One's friends! Carole!
Thank you. Will you be long?

TREVOR HOLLINGSHEAD: But you're very rich
   aren't you?

SIR GEOFFREY KENDLE: I'm always being robbed.
   Will you be long?

TREVOR HOLLINGSHEAD: What?

SIR GEOFFREY KENDLE: Standing there.

TREVOR HOLLINGSHEAD: Hours. Will you be long?

*He shouts into the radio, grins,
'whats' to himself,
listens to a reply perhaps, perhaps
not and goes on to shout, looking at
SIR GEOFFREY:*

Sir Geoffrey wants to know how long you're
going to be lining up this ridiculous shot.

SIR GEOFFREY KENDLE: No no, don't say me!

TREVOR HOLLINGSHEAD: Don't you want to know?

SIR GEOFFREY KENDLE: Please, don't blame me
for it.

TREVOR HOLLINGSHEAD: What? They won't be
long.

*He grins. He could be thought to be
shy. He isn't.*

SIR GEOFFREY KENDLE: You thrive on adversity.

TREVOR HOLLINGSHEAD: Do you really think so?

SIR GEOFFREY KENDLE: I do.

TREVOR HOLLINGSHEAD: I don't. Really.

SIR GEOFFREY KENDLE: You give that impression.

TREVOR HOLLINGSHEAD: Then it's the wrong
impression.
What about your friend?

SIR GEOFFREY KENDLE: Poor Dotty, I wonder
if there's anything we can do...

TREVOR HOLLINGSHEAD: Your friend Dotty D'Orsay.

SIR GEOFFREY KENDLE: Well, yes.

TREVOR HOLLINGSHEAD: Shouldn't you choose
your friends more carefully?

SIR GEOFFREY KENDLE: Oh I do. Dotty is an
old friend you see, before one did anything
so grand as to choose one's chums,
you see,
when chums just happened, came about rather
than came around... poor Dotty.

TREVOR HOLLINGSHEAD: Is he whining?

SIR GEOFFREY KENDLE: He's awfully upset.

TREVOR HOLLINGSHEAD: I can't bear his whining, he's so contemptible.

SIR GEOFFREY KENDLE: Yes he is contemptible. It means so much to him you see.

TREVOR HOLLINGSHEAD: What does?

SIR GEOFFREY KENDLE: This film.

TREVOR HOLLINGSHEAD: You wouldn't think so, the way he behaves.

SIR GEOFFREY KENDLE: No you wouldn't.

TREVOR HOLLINGSHEAD: He's not cheap, I can tell you.

SIR GEOFFREY KENDLE: What?

TREVOR HOLLINGSHEAD: But he's very nasty.

SIR GEOFFREY KENDLE: He has a following in America.

TREVOR HOLLINGSHEAD: I'm not surprised, are you?

SIR GEOFFREY KENDLE: Well you see, he can sing and dance, awfully useful.

TREVOR HOLLINGSHEAD: You can sing and dance.

SIR GEOFFREY KENDLE: No no!

TREVOR HOLLINGSHEAD: Yes you can.

SIR GEOFFREY KENDLE: No, really.

Panic in his eyes, he grips his chair and checks his exit.

TREVOR HOLLINGSHEAD: You can do anything.

SIR GEOFFREY KENDLE: Oh I wish that were
true, I wouldn't be cheap.

TREVOR HOLLINGSHEAD: Look at all the people
who can sing and dance.

SIR GEOFFREY KENDLE: Yes yes, but not as
many as at one time.

TREVOR HOLLINGSHEAD: That's because it's
so boring.

SIR GEOFFREY KENDLE: Come now, some of them
were charming. I mean look at those first,
those early musicals...

TREVOR HOLLINGSHEAD: Boring.

SIR GEOFFREY KENDLE: He rides terribly well.

TREVOR HOLLINGSHEAD: So do the whole of
the Turkish Cavalry.

SIR GEOFFREY KENDLE: Yes, aren't they superb?
Where are they?

TREVOR HOLLINGSHEAD: They've gone.

SIR GEOFFREY KENDLE: Dotty is terribly reliable
in an emergency.

*SIR GEOFFREY KENDLE cannot believe he has
said what he has said,
with the conviction he has said it,
so he says it again:*

He's very reliable in an emergency. He can
be relied upon. There's Penelope you see,
she's always around to keep an eye on him,
but he's settled down recently,
he knows it's very important he should
do something worthwhile... in an absolute
emergency he is most reliable...

TREVOR HOLLINGSHEAD: Do you really believe that?

SIR GEOFFREY KENDLE: Yes I do, I do. I do.
I really do. I do, I do.

TREVOR HOLLINGSHEAD: Have you ever tried telling him to fuck off?

SIR GEOFFREY KENDLE: It comes to mind.

TREVOR HOLLINGSHEAD: You ought to.

SIR GEOFFREY KENDLE: He wouldn't though,
and there you've been unpleasant for no
reason.
He's truly contrite.

TREVOR HOLLINGSHEAD: He always is.

SIR GEOFFREY KENDLE: I know, that's one of
the nicer things about him.
That comes to mind.

TREVOR HOLLINGSHEAD: He's just boring.

SIR GEOFFREY KENDLE: Oh he's very boring, you
see he tries so hard.
Is it true you've sent him off the set? I
mean are you going to send him home?

TREVOR HOLLINGSHEAD: What? I told him not
to say anything.

SIR GEOFFREY KENDLE: Why?

TREVOR HOLLINGSHEAD: Why? Because I didn't
want a fuss.

SIR GEOFFREY KENDLE: I mean at this stage
of the film, will it not cause untold
complications, I mean will you take out
all his scenes, I mean, why?

TREVOR HOLLINGSHEAD: Because he exposed himself.

SIR GEOFFREY KENDLE: Did he?

TREVOR HOLLINGSHEAD: Because he flashed his chopper at the Hon. Ursula.

SIR GEOFFREY KENDLE: Did he? Did she say he did?

TREVOR HOLLINGSHEAD: She said it wasn't very nice.

SIR GEOFFREY KENDLE: Oh it isn't. Do we know her?

TREVOR HOLLINGSHEAD: I know her, her father is very important, and useful. She's the Honourable Ursula Marjoribanks.

SIR GEOFFREY KENDLE: Marshbanks.

TREVOR HOLLINGSHEAD: I prefer Marjoribanks, don't you?

SIR GEOFFREY KENDLE: Yes I do, but it isn't right.

TREVOR HOLLINGSHEAD: But isn't it funnier?

SIR GEOFFREY KENDLE: Very funny.

TREVOR HOLLINGSHEAD: What?

Laughing, that braying laugh and slap of his legs, running on the spot without moving his heels and toes from the ground, rubbing his hands up and down his thigh.

I mean, Marjoribanks?

SIR GEOFFREY KENDLE: Might I talk to her do you think?

TREVOR HOLLINGSHEAD: No.

SIR GEOFFREY KENDLE: I mean if you think it
would do any good.
What is she going to do?
I mean, we all know Dotty gets tired
and does these things,
since I can't remember. I think it's very
sad the way he automatically flees to his
flies in times of stress,
that's why I always cast him in armour if I
possibly can, or tights, not that... I
remember At Elsinore in that dreadful down-
pour of rain,
that awful hotel where we eventually opened,
actually it was quite a nice hotel
and the Danes were charming;
Dotty was arrested twice, once for the
usual thing and once for hiding in a
wardrobe and watching men at work,
but he was awfully good, acted us all off
the stage;
who was that comic who used to do a
similar thing in Bradford and bring the
house down?
Might I talk to her?

TREVOR HOLLINGSHEAD: No. She's upset enough.

SIR GEOFFREY KENDLE: Oh surely, this day and
age!

TREVOR HOLLINGSHEAD: I'm sick and tired of
your precious friend.

SIR GEOFFREY KENDLE: I've explained that.
We're only chums because we always have
been chums.

TREVOR HOLLINGSHEAD: Now's your chance to
rid yourself of him.

SIR GEOFFREY KENDLE: I'd love to, but he's
 so down.

TREVOR HOLLINGSHEAD: I don't want to talk
 about him.

SIR GEOFFREY KENDLE: What about poor Penelope!
 I'm very fond of her, have you seen
 her black eye?

TREVOR HOLLINGSHEAD: No, I've heard about
 it, is it awful?

SIR GEOFFREY KENDLE: Terribly attractive,
 the merest smudge.

TREVOR HOLLINGSHEAD: Super.

SIR GEOFFREY KENDLE: She came out of it
 very well. What does 'Hair in the gate' mean?
 Will you lose her scenes?

TREVOR HOLLINGSHEAD: Why?

SIR GEOFFREY KENDLE: No reason why you should,
 I'm sure she's awfully good and then you can
 say you expect better from Dotty,
 he is to pull his socks up,
 and why doesn't he start by saying sorry to
 his wife and putting all that right.
 I'm sure he wouldn't mind. In fact I know
 he would do it like a shot, he loves
 abasing himself,
 does it awfully well and sincere as Moses,
 and you see Miss Marshbanks might like to
 be present, join with us, Marjoribanks.
 Very funny.

 A noise from the radio.

 Do you want me now?

TREVOR HOLLINGSHEAD: No, you sit still for
 a while, make the buggers wait.

SIR GEOFFREY KENDLE: What do you think of
it for an idea?

TREVOR HOLLINGSHEAD: I think it's a very
bad idea because Penelope is going to stay.

SIR GEOFFREY KENDLE: Would she be likely to?

TREVOR HOLLINGSHEAD: Yes, I'm going to see
she does.

SIR GEOFFREY KENDLE: Dotty will kill himself.

TREVOR HOLLINGSHEAD: Oh don't be silly, he's
too much of a coward.

SIR GEOFFREY KENDLE: I always thought he was
very brave.

TREVOR HOLLINGSHEAD: He's not.

SIR GEOFFREY KENDLE: No.
Under that rough, tough exterior there
beats the heart of a little old lady.

TREVOR HOLLINGSHEAD: What?
You are funny Geoffrey, I wish I could say
the same for your friend.

SIR GEOFFREY KENDLE: Don't keep calling him
my friend,
it puts such a responsibility on one.
I shan't say any more. I have surely
done my best...

*SIR GEOFFREY KENDLE settles into the
chair with a sigh, a gesture with
his hands, a look up into the sky
for a witness. TREVOR HOLLINGSHEAD is
grinning, waiting, he asks:*

TREVOR HOLLINGSHEAD: What else about your
friend?

SIR GEOFFREY KENDLE: He didn't get shingles
   when everybody else did.

*Mournfully, the memory of his own
shingles very painful. TREVOR hoots
with laughter and states:*

TREVOR HOLLINGSHEAD: Oh Sir Geoffrey, you
   are marvellous. You are such good value.

*SIR GEOFFREY KENDLE suddenly angry
gets to his feet and strides across
the front. Stops, strides back to
his chair and stands behind it.
TREVOR grinning, watching him.*

What?

SIR GEOFFREY KENDLE: Look, are you going
   to need me?

TREVOR HOLLINGSHEAD: Yes love. We're lining
   up a shot for you.
   Sit down.

SIR GEOFFREY KENDLE: I am not good value
   as you call it.

TREVOR HOLLINGSHEAD: Yes you are, I think
   you're marvellous.
   You're angry Geoffrey, I've never seen
   you angry before.

SIR GEOFFREY KENDLE: Please don't worry
   about it.

TREVOR HOLLINGSHEAD: But I do, I want you
   to be happy.

SIR GEOFFREY KENDLE: Yes.
   I want you to understand this, Dotty will
   go to pieces if you chuck him off this
   film.

TREVOR HOLLINGSHEAD: Sir Geoffrey, you've
got to understand you are more use to us
than a hundred such as Mr Laurence D'Orsay,
and you are good value...

SIR GEOFFREY KENDLE: I suppose I am if I'm
cheap.

TREVOR HOLLINGSHEAD: Do you want more?

SIR GEOFFREY KENDLE: More...?

TREVOR HOLLINGSHEAD: Sit down.

SIR GEOFFREY KENDLE: What do you mean, more?

TREVOR HOLLINGSHEAD: Do you?

SIR GEOFFREY KENDLE: I don't think so.

TREVOR HOLLINGSHEAD: Because you can have
what you want.

SIR GEOFFREY KENDLE: I am more than happy
with what I've got, thank you very much.
I hate all this have-whatever-you-want
lark you get on films,
you all do it, and you all do mean it,
you all do mean what you say, upon bare
friendship as if...

TREVOR HOLLINGSHEAD: Super.

SIR GEOFFREY KENDLE: Suppose I said there
were several things you could give, as if
you could... these sickly sweets the
Americans sell, I've seen so many young
and promising actors ruined;
they can't keep it up you see when they
go home so they loll and mope and wait
for the car to come...

TREVOR HOLLINGSHEAD: I mean more money.

SIR GEOFFREY KENDLE: I know you do. Do
    you?

*TREVOR HOLLINGSHEAD hoots again and
this time SIR GEOFFREY KENDLE smiles
with him, approving.*

TREVOR HOLLINGSHEAD: Now you can't say
    that wasn't funny, you meant that to be
    funny.

SIR GEOFFREY KENDLE: Yes I did hope.
    But you see what I mean about gorging on
    it don't you?

TREVOR HOLLINGSHEAD: It's not free, we all
    have to pay.

SIR GEOFFREY KENDLE: Oh don't be silly.
    That's silly and invented out of guilt,
    Trevor, what do you pay?

TREVOR HOLLINGSHEAD: I get so tired.

SIR GEOFFREY KENDLE: Nonsense.

TREVOR HOLLINGSHEAD: I do.

SIR GEOFFREY KENDLE: Absolute lies. Do you?

TREVOR HOLLINGSHEAD: Yes.
    Exhausted. Don't you?

*He laughs, grins at SIR GEOFFREY
and up at the tower.*

SIR GEOFFREY KENDLE: I do, wonderfully.
    You know, you're one of the happiest
    men I know, apart, that is, from myself.
    At any rate, you appear to be and
    appearances six weeks in are rarely

deceptive... tired or no.
To be so young and be so happy is marvellous.
And attractive.

TREVOR HOLLINGSHEAD: What?

*TREVOR HOLLINGSHEAD shades his eyes
although he can see SIR GEOFFREY KENDLE
perfectly well.*

SIR GEOFFREY KENDLE: You must find it so?

TREVOR HOLLINGSHEAD: Is it?

SIR GEOFFREY KENDLE: Oh madly.

*Enter BERNIE THE VOLT an inch, to
squint at the sun a moment through his
pan glass, and squint at TREVOR and SIR
GEOFFREY KENDLE on the down glance.
SIR GEOFFREY continues:*

We both know it, look at our mothy hangers-
on. Your grotesques with their cock-like
hammers and magic windows, squinting at
the sun and seeing you...

*They both look at BERNIE THE VOLT
who squints again at the sun in the sky,
grins and shouts off up the tower.*

BERNIE: Fucking sun eh?

SIR GEOFFREY KENDLE: Every other director
I've worked with has been festooned with
squinters, why haven't you got one?
Trevor?

TREVOR HOLLINGSHEAD: I can see quite well
without one, I don't need one.
Do you want one?
Bernie, you are to give your pan glass to
Sir Geoffrey. He ought to have one.

BERNIE: Guv?

SIR GEOFFREY KENDLE: Oh no.

*TREVOR HOLLINGSHEAD takes the pan
glass and cord from around BERNIE's
neck and dangles
it at SIR GEOFFREY saying:*

TREVOR HOLLINGSHEAD: Yes, I want you to
have one.

Dropping it over SIR GEOFFREY's head.

SIR GEOFFREY KENDLE: But what about Bernie,
isn't it his badge of office?

TREVOR HOLLINGSHEAD: It suits you. You can
have it for when you direct a film.
Doesn't it suit him Bernie? Now you want
a view-finder. Bernie, get a view-finder.
You ought to direct films,
why don't you direct your own films,
Geoffrey? Everybody should direct their
own films, it's very easy.

SIR GEOFFREY KENDLE: I'm sure you're wrong.

TREVOR HOLLINGSHEAD: I'm not. It used not
to be, but it's very easy now.

Exit BERNIE to procure a view-finder.

Didn't you know that? Everybody directs
their own films now. The only difficulty
is getting the money, that's still very
difficult.

SIR GEOFFREY KENDLE: I'm sure you're right.

*Peering through the pan glass,
down the hill and up into the sky.
Enter BERNIE with a view-finder.*

TREVOR HOLLINGSHEAD invests SIR
GEOFFREY KENDLE with the view-finder,
holding it so that the actor can
squint through it. Altering the adjustment,
SIR GEOFFREY exclaims:

There's Dotty, I can just see his head and
his shoulders sitting there all alone,
now that is sadness,
his little shoulders,
his little old shoulders,
were I a film director I would catch those
frail childlike shoulders...

TREVOR HOLLINGSHEAD: If you directed your
own films you could have your precious
Dotty in every one of them.

SIR GEOFFREY KENDLE: Oh!

He drops the view-finder quickly.
TREVOR hoots with laughter and asks
the hovering BERNIE:

TREVOR HOLLINGSHEAD: Couldn't he Bernie?

SIR GEOFFREY KENDLE: What a thought!

TREVOR HOLLINGSHEAD: What!

Enter BRYAN DAVID.
He is not sure. He hesitates before
advancing in front of the reflectors.

SIR GEOFFREY KENDLE: Bryan, what are you
doing?

TREVOR HOLLINGSHEAD: Ah Bryan, there you
are.

SIR GEOFFREY KENDLE: Why don't you go and
talk to Dotty, sit with him?

BRYAN DAVID: Oh no. Why?

SIR GEOFFREY KENDLE: No. It's awful the
    way nobody will. Everbody leaves him
    alone at lunchtime and in the evenings,
    will not share a car with him to come
    out in the mornings,
    with him,
    go back at the end of the day...

BRYAN DAVID: That's not the way to use a
    pan glass, Trevor, is it?

SIR GEOFFREY KENDLE: Is it not?

    He is peering throught the pan glass
    at the amphitheatre below, he looks
    over the top of it at BRYAN DAVID.

TREVOR HOLLINGSHEAD: What do you know
    about it Bryan?

BRYAN DAVID: You look at the sky with it,
    at the clouds and the sun, that's what
    Bernie does.

SIR GEOFFREY KENDLE: Always?

TREVOR HOLLINGSHEAD: Not always. Why aren't
    you in costume?

BRYAN DAVID: Are you black and white or
    colour, Sir Geoffrey? Because it depends...

SIR GEOFFREY KENDLE: I'm colour, at my
    age one feels the cold so much more.

TREVOR HOLLINGSHEAD: Why aren't you in
    costume Bryan David?

BRYAN DAVID: I wasn't called, love.

TREVOR HOLLINGSHEAD: I want you in this.

BRYAN DAVID: I wasn't called.

TREVOR HOLLINGSHEAD: You should have been.
Go and get your horse.

SIR GEOFFREY KENDLE: Oh dear. You don't
mean it.

BRYAN DAVID: Bernie, get my horse brought
up will you? What about yours Geoffrey?

SIR GEOFFREY KENDLE: Oh dear.

TREVOR HOLLINGSHEAD: Don't you want to be
on your horse?

SIR GEOFFREY KENDLE: Really, I don't mind.

TREVOR HOLLINGSHEAD: Sir Geoffrey doesn't
want his horse.

SIR GEOFFREY KENDLE: Please...

TREVOR HOLLINGSHEAD: You can stand on a box
if you like Geoffrey.

SIR GEOFFREY KENDLE: How terribly kind of
you, how marvellous, I've got a sore bum
you see Bryan. (*Delighted.*)

TREVOR HOLLINGSHEAD: You can have a box
as well Bryan.

BRYAN DAVID: No.

TREVOR HOLLINGSHEAD: Don't argue.

BRYAN DAVID: I mean, I can be mounted
surely?

TREVOR HOLLINGSHEAD: Can you? Sir Geoffrey
wants you on a box.

BRYAN DAVID: I'm sure you're wrong.

SIR GEOFFREY KENDLE: Please, no...

TREVOR HOLLINGSHEAD: Bernie?

BERNIE: Guv?

TREVOR HOLLINGSHEAD: Don't take any notice
of Mr David, you are to get two horse
boxes, for Sir Geoffrey and Mr Bryan David.

BRYAN DAVID: Oh no, surely!

TREVOR HOLLINGSHEAD: What?
You can paint Mr David's box a dashing white.

Exit TREVOR HOLLINGSHEAD.
To climb the tower, a final bray and
a grin as he goes.

What?

Exit BERNIE THE VOLT with a wave of his
hammer.
BRYAN DAVID calls after TREVOR:

BRYAN DAVID: I'm sorry Trevor, but I'm not
going to do it. Do you think I should refuse
Sir Geoffrey?

SIR GEOFFREY KENDLE: I never do.

BRYAN DAVID: It's so bloody silly you see
when I can ride perfectly well,
so humiliating to have to stand on a box.
Is he queer do you know?

SIR GEOFFREY KENDLE: Oh come now, I've
seen Douglas Fairbanks on a box,
he always managed terribly well,
if you will play dashing parts you must
expect to end up on a box some time.
Look at Dotty, he rides beautifully

and he's been thrown off the film,
you may thank your lucky stars you
only end up riding a box,
you might get to like it, I love it and
I'm not in the least humiliated, do
you know they call my fiendish beast Arkle?
I can't think why unless they mean to intimidate me...

BRYAN DAVID: Do you think he is?

SIR GEOFFREY KENDLE: I know he's not, but
I just hope that he doesn't think he is,
I couldn't cope if he took it into his
head to win the Grand National or whatever
it was his namesake did.
He won't, he's full of drugs I'm pleased
to say but he's still got too much life
in him to please me entirely.

BRYAN DAVID: No, I mean Trevor, is he queer?

SIR GEOFFREY KENDLE: I beg your pardon?

BRYAN DAVID: I think he is.

SIR GEOFFREY KENDLE: Why don't you ask him?
I would.

BRYAN DAVID: I can't stand them.

SIR GEOFFREY KENDLE: Just as well you're
not then isn't it?

BRYAN DAVID: Oh I'm not.

SIR GEOFFREY KENDLE: How nice to be so sure.

BRYAN DAVID: Do you think I am?

SIR GEOFFREY KENDLE: Do you think you are?

BRYAN DAVID: Oh I know I'm not for God's
sake. I mean do you think I am?

SIR GEOFFREY KENDLE: Is it important to you, it's never been important to me, I mean is it important?

BRYAN DAVID: Of course it is Sir Geoffrey, I want to get married and get out of this facile existence.

SIR GEOFFREY KENDLE: Oh congratulations by the way, I hope you'll be very happy.

BRYAN DAVID: Thank you.

SIR GEOFFREY KENDLE: Penelope told me, I hope you don't mind?

BRYAN DAVID: Did she tell you that I find it impossible to develop a satisfactory relationship with any mature human being beyond the immediate gratification of my desires, I mean I can screw them... I mean that's all right.

SIR GEOFFREY KENDLE: No she didn't tell me that.

BRYAN DAVID: Oh yes.

SIR GEOFFREY KENDLE: Never mind, here comes your box and mine. I hope they're compatible.

Enter BERNIE THE VOLT with two rostrums, about four foot high. He places them near the batten mark. The two actors look at them. BERNIE grins and waves his hammer from his crutch.

BRYAN DAVID: I don't think I can face it.

SIR GEOFFREY KENDLE: Bryan, I'm terribly sorry.

SIR GEOFFREY KENDLE stops on his way
to mount his box,
closes his eyes, puts out a hand to
touch BRYAN and strikes his forehead
once with the flat of his other hand
asking abjectly:

How can you forgive me?
I have just this moment realized on
hearing the word relationship,
there, I said to myself there, an
American involved,
relationships, you can't know the brown
grey-haired flannel-suited earnest hours
I've skirted every possible relationship
before leaping log fires off Curzon Street
where they all settle,
have you noticed?
Aren't they quaint with their log fires,
books, bronzes and relationships?
Do you have any idea how Americans in
London come to be the colour they are,
brown? Is it brown? Surely it's not brown?
No, it's not brown and it's not yellow and
it isn't always slap so you can't put a
number to it...
How healthy it makes them
look but how vulnerable...
... are they not quaint?
But my dear boy, did you love her
desperately, your American? The Blue Mosque
was a sweet thought... dear me, here I am
going on about them as if I didn't know we
all have reason to be grateful to them,
my fault entirely,
Penelope did warn me it was off, why you
were drinking desperately and letting

yourself go,
no soul so near,
I keep being nudged by Trolius don't you?
Have you managed to see Troy?
They tell me you can't, the military still
there... after all these years,
which military I ask?
They can't still be... Bryan my dear fellow,
how can you ever forgive me for rubbing
salt, will you take ever so long to
get over her, do you think? Will you
want to talk about it?

BRYAN DAVID: Oh yes.

SIR GEOFFREY KENDLE: Ah, I shouldn't, it
never helps and often hinders...

BRYAN DAVID: I hate being the odd man
out, it's happening more and more.

SIR GEOFFREY KENDLE: It is?

BRYAN DAVID: You would think nobody cared
about love any more in the truest sense,
that of a man for a woman... of course I
know I'm not bent but I would hate it to
be thought I was,
for any reason, I feel a ridiculous
compulsion to prove myself, I mean do
you think I ride well?

SIR GEOFFREY KENDLE: Ah! I'm no judge.

BRYAN DAVID: I'm an excellent horseman.

SIR GEOFFREY KENDLE: That proves it then.

BRYAN DAVID: Do you think I'm a good sabre?

SIR GEOFFREY KENDLE: I'm sure you are, but
then I'm really no judge,

the most I can do is cut parry thrust
for the last bit of Hamlet, one two three,
on two three, I'm sure you are... there
you are, you see, very manly.

BRYAN DAVID: I regarded it as a challenge.

SIR GEOFFREY KENDLE: A very good way to
approach your work...

BRYAN DAVID: So you see how it is, I'm not
going to be able to get onto that box!

SIR GEOFFREY KENDLE: Come now, Bernie will
make a back for you, or better still let's
do it together while nobody's looking,
hold my hand and we'll do it together.

BRYAN DAVID: No, you're very kind but I
can't do it.

*BERNIE makes a step with his hands
and hoists SIR GEOFFREY KENDLE up
and onto the box,
he stands looking down into the
amphitheatre.*

SIR GEOFFREY KENDLE: Oh come now, there's
a marvellous view Bryan.
Thank you Bernie, these tight trousers
don't help.
Oh I can see Dotty sitting there all alone.

*Exit BERNIE THE VOLT to the remark
from SIR GEOFFREY:*

Exit Thersites, don't you think? Enter
another part of the field not so well
lit. Poor Trevor, that's where all the
drama is... off the set.
Are you coming up?

If you're not coming up why don't you go
sit with Dotty a while, out of kindness.

BRYAN DAVID: I don't know what I should
do. I cannot bring myself to mount that
box. You see I feel it's wrong, I know it's
wrong for the film.

SIR GEOFFREY KENDLE: Penelope should be with
him when he's so smitten,
why isn't she sitting with him holding his
hand or whatever, I mean she's a kind
person, I've seen her be very kind.
It is rather high.

BRYAN DAVID: I shall be the laughing stock
of the unit, Trevor... Trevor!

SIR GEOFFREY KENDLE: It's not terribly
solid is it?

BRYAN DAVID: Bernie, where is Trevor?

SIR GEOFFREY KENDLE: I think you'll find
that he's up the tower with his camera.
Should you bother him?

BRYAN DAVID: Bernie, where are you?

SIR GEOFFREY KENDLE: I think Bernie is rather busy
too...

BRYAN DAVID: Bernie, will you inform Mr
Hollingshead that I refuse to mount that
box when there is a perfectly good horse
available... ?

*Enter BERNIE, his head round one of the
reflectors, carbons in his hands,
wearing gloves,
a hand to his ear.*

BERNIE: Yes guv?

BRYAN DAVID: Ah, there you are Bernie! You
may inform the director that I am walking
off the set...

SIR GEOFFREY KENDLE: Ah, there you are
Bernie...

BRYAN DAVID: Just tell him that will you?

Exit BRYAN DAVID down the hill.
Exit BERNIE THE VOLT without comment,
his hand back behind the reflectors,
leaving SIR GEOFFREY KENDLE standing
alone on his box.
A moment of silence.

SIR GEOFFREY KENDLE: Do you know, I'm not
going to get off this box? I'm not.

He casts round for a way
down, tries to step on to the top of
the other box,
finds it more wobbly than his own,
it creaks.
An angry glance at where he can see
TREVOR and another attempt at a call,
strangled in his throat,
he tries to go down on one knee,
his trousers too tight,
he fumbles at the buttons of his braces,
his trousers still too tight,
his sword caught up in his legs, he tries
to slide down the side of the box,
loses his nerve,
stands up again and fumbles at the buckle
of his swordbelt.
A scratching of nails on gold thread.

He shouts:

Trevor! Trevor Hollingshead, please.

Silence.

SIR GEOFFREY sucks a fingernail torn
by his buckle, bites it off,
tries again to get the swordbelt off.
And then he closes his eyes in an
attempt to calm himself,
eyes tight shut he sways a little on
the box, putting out a hand to steady
himself against nothing,
deep breathing,
opens his eyes quickly as he seems
about to fall, doesn't fall.
Closes his eyes again. Deep calming
breathing. Then he says quietly almost
a whisper, like an actor running through a
speech to start with and then louder
and stronger:

"I have been here,
in the night a child came and
took my hand – a young woman, gentle
a sad beauty with large and wondrous
beautiful eyes, hunger,
she took me into a nightmare
of horses and a cannon,
my sword cardboard,
my legs in mud to the thigh,
I fought so hard,
I could not think of movements
and evolutions, I could not have
proved a company,
I hacked and slashed,
my sword would not cut and I had

not a command I could utter, I was
as a woman, I was not accoutred and
I was alone in the midst of savage
carnage the like I hope never to
witness ever again, ever, never.
A child hanged on a hook, I see
the marks of his drumming heels,
rags of cloth tied across the door
by women in terror,
they hold the butchers one brief
moment before they are in and at
their awful work,
sepoys turn away – they will not
look as butchers from the bazaar
hack and batter with their swords
in the end mere bludgeons,
twice they come out to sharpen.
To stand this siege
to see their men die in war,
to surrender, be given a through
and then be tortured in this way,
slaughtered, treacherously, as cattle;
they smiled some of them in ghastly
coquettish manner, pulled down their
underthings and offered themselves
for the lives of their children.
They cried, but there was none to
hear, even unto the Lord they
cried – but He answered them not.
I stood ignored,
a spirit at the real fleshing.
I fought,
my fists a puff of dust,
and I heard my guns, I heard
my army coming.
I was at the gates of Cawnpore
with my army, asleep."

Enter BERNIE THE VOLT during this,
carrying a stand with a French flag
clamped to it. He places the stand
in front of one of the 'brutes',
walks round the back of the reflector
and the 'brute' fizzes into life.
Wearing asbestos gloves BERNIE adjusts
the carbons in the 'brute',
comes back and stands near to the
metal stand with its French flag,
squinting up into the sky through a
pan glass.
SIR GEOFFREY KENDLE opens his eyes
and looks straight up into the muslin
filters.

Not a cloud in the sky, an impossible sky.

BERNIE: Fucking sun.

SIR GEOFFREY KENDLE: Don't say that.

BERNIE: Fucking sun.

SIR GEOFFREY KENDLE: I thought you'd gone off and left me.

BERNIE: They're back, the fucking Turks.

SIR GEOFFREY KENDLE: Oh good. Where have they been?

BERNIE: The army? Shoot some fucking students it seems.

SIR GEOFFREY KENDLE: Surely not.

BERNIE: Wouldn't surprise me, the whole fucking country is seething.

SIR GEOFFREY KENDLE: Really? Everybody is very nice to me.

BERNIE: What did you say guv?

SIR GEOFFREY KENDLE: Who?

BERNIE: Up the tower.

SIR GEOFFREY KENDLE: I'm sorry I wasn't listening.

BERNIE: Do me a favour, you're nearer
than me, God bless you guv.

*He gives his wireless to SIR GEOFFREY
who holds it gingerly.*

SIR GEOFFREY KENDLE: Yes.
Those muslin swags up there, like the
banners of Genghis Khan, the flags of Timurlane,
dread flags smeared to blot the sun, or washing,
somebody's washing up from the Ganges
hung to dry. Have you been to India, Bernie?

BERNIE: Yes guv, I don't reckon the
fucking poverty though.

SIR GEOFFREY KENDLE: Nothing to do with you is it?

BERNIE: You can't help noticing it can you?

*A noise from the wireless, SIR GEOFFREY listens
without comprehension and then says:*

SIR GEOFFREY KENDLE: Up the tower, something
to do with the Chinese.

BERNIE: God bless you, make it Chinese.

*Which he does, slanting the French flag
on the metal stand to make it Chinese.
Coming back to stand under the rostrum
and squint up at the sky, he says:*

Funny you should mention Temudjyn.

SIR GEOFFREY KENDLE: Did I? Could you give
me your hand?
I thought I'd been forgotten.

Holding out a hand for BERNIE to help
him down,
BERNIE doesn't, he nods and continues:

BERNIE: Funny that, I've been meaning to
ask your advice on that, on Temudjyn.

SIR GEOFFREY KENDLE: I beg your pardon?

BERNIE: Otherwise known as Genghis Khan,
that was his real name actually,
Temudjyn, I thought you would have known
that. It's got everything you know, horses,
epic landscapes, bags of blood and sacks
full of tit, do you know they wore fuck-all
under their clothes until Queen Victoria?
So that puts us right for tit,
I hold the motion picture rights to Genghis
Khan, it's not commonly known.
I was given them for my work on Trevor's
first picture,
and he gave me a Rolls Royce. I got a
contract all square. Genghis Khan.

SIR GEOFFREY KENDLE: Hasn't it been done?

BERNIE: No, not properly, fucking hell it's
a bramah done right, a great narrative story.
I want him to have no eyelids see, fantastic.
You know what I mean don't you? He knows
what I mean. (*He shouts off.*) What?

SIR GEOFFREY KENDLE: I'm sorry?

BERNIE: Second unit. They got a split, tell
them they got a split...

SIR GEOFFREY KENDLE: (*Into wireless*) Bernie says they've
got a split...

BERNIE: God bless you guv.

SIR GEOFFREY KENDLE: Follow the money?
whatever that may mean.

BERNIE: What I said, didn't I? Follow the
money. Follow the fucking money says
Trevor.

He repeats loudly sotto voce off:

Trev says you are to follow the money.
That's you guv.

SIR GEOFFREY KENDLE: Is it? I wish I
knew what we were doing.

BERNIE: Day for night isn't it?

SIR GEOFFREY KENDLE: I'm sure it is but
am I meant to say anything?
I should be saying my long speech I do
believe, I hope I know it.

BERNIE: They've cut that, that's out.

SIR GEOFFREY KENDLE: What?

BERNIE: Stand by.

SIR GEOFFREY KENDLE: (*Into wireless.*) What,
what? Trevor, I really must know what I'm
supposed to do, to say.

BERNIE: Another thing I wanted to ask
you, with Larry, I mean do you admire him
as an actor?

SIR GEOFFREY KENDLE: Did he say anything?

*Looking up into the tower, his hands
over his eyes,
bleating without any real hope of
being heard: 'Trevor! Trevor!'*

BERNIE: I do. I think he's the finest
fucking actor in the world today, in the
motion picture industry today, do you?

SIR GEOFFREY KENDLE: Yes he is, absolutely
marvellous. Who? Which Larry?

BERNIE: I do, sincerely. Do you?

SIR GEOFFREY KENDLE: I do, I do, who?

BERNIE: I'm prepared to fill him in for
Genghis, I've got him pencilled. Look, you
know him, right, you tell him I'll take a
chance on him, thousands wouldn't, but not
to put too fine a point on it this motion
picture is a labour of love with me,
I mean that sincerely. I can wait see, I've
had this property for years waiting for the
right actor... stand by,
now you tell him that will you, as a friend
because we all know he's got a fucking drink
problem hasn't he?

SIR GEOFFREY KENDLE: Dotty! He's not a Larry.

BERNIE: *Sus* now. Will you do that guv?

SIR GEOFFREY KENDLE: Do what? Do what
Trevor?

BERNIE: Chat him, tell him I'm prepared to
offer him Genghis Khan.

SIR GEOFFREY KENDLE: You want me to talk
to Dotty?

BERNIE: No bullshit, this will make
motion picture history, *sus* now.

*He changes his voice, makes it deeper
like an auctioneer getting near the*

*top of the bidding and says, ducking
down to a squat behind the box:*

Absolute quiet please.

SIR GEOFFREY KENDLE: (*Into wireless.*) Do you
want the long Cawnpore speech, Trevor?

BERNIE: That's been cut.

SIR GEOFFREY KENDLE: Trevor?

*Looking up at the tower, SIR GEOFFREY
KENDLE waits to be told. The tower
shakes a little,
a voice says something like 'speed',
but one can't be sure. The only real
sound is the tinkle of a goat bell
quite near, BERNIE THE VOLT grins
evilly and brandishes his hammer. He
says in his loudest sotto voce:*

BERNIE: *Sus solem lutven* that fucking goat
or I'll have it kebab, little squares like
Oxo. Absolute quiet please.

SIR GEOFFREY KENDLE: Did Trevor say what I
was to do?

BERNIE: Here we go then.

SIR GEOFFREY KENDLE: Oh!

BERNIE: Cut!

SIR GEOFFREY KENDLE: What?

BERNIE: You er, you er ever in Putney? Do
you get round that way at all?

*BERNIE embarrassed,
looking over his shoulder at SIR GEOFFREY KENDLE*

who has never seen BERNIE blush
before, a shy flick of his hammer as he
goes on to say:

Come round to tea when we get back. Do you
good to relax with a real family,
we're very ordinary, the house is Georgian
you'll like it, one afternoon?
Meet the family, they'd be chuffed.

SIR GEOFFREY KENDLE: Tea? How very kind but...

BERNIE: Any day but Sunday. I won't have
Sunday fucked up,
only day you get isn't it? Look in your
diary when you get back for a date...
Sus now, here we go again, stand by...

Says BERNIE THE VOLT ducking down
behind a reflector and in his deep voice
as another 'brute' spits to life:

Let's have absolute fucking quiet if you please,
sus solem lutven the stirrups.

Faces, dozens of them, appear to edge
the reflectors,
watching with interest SIR GEOFFREY
KENDLE and an approach of noise,
a distant rumble and a far-away shout
of panic,
then blazing flare of light from yet
another 'brute' and another, SIR GEOFFREY
KENDLE's shout echoes the panic:

SIR GEOFFREY KENDLE: I don't know what to do,
I don't know what you want me to do!
I have been here,
in the night a child came and
took my hand – a young woman, gentle
a sad beauty...

He offers without conviction to the
oncoming noise.
The curtain comes down.

While the curtain is down.
Noise, noise, noise and light of horse,
foot and elephant engaged in the walls
of the auditorium in wide-screen colours.

Scene 2

The curtain rises.
Scene the same. Discovered solus, SIR
GEOFFREY KENDLE standing on the box
holding up his sword knot out of
harm's way, clouded by settling dust.
He coughs, and asks, though he hardly
dare:

SIR GEOFFREY KENDLE: Was that all right?
I thought I transposed a line.

Silence but for the 'ping' of cooling
metal. The actor puts out a hand for
help, he wants to get down. Asks:

Do you think I could get down now?

No answer.

Actually I'm not at all sure I said the
right speech, was that the right speech?

Silence.

I'm terribly sorry, my fault entirely.
Would you like me to start at the beginning
again, Trevor? If you could possibly tell
me what I did last time, I'd be more than
pleased to do it again... might I sit down
while you're getting the animals together?

Still no answer. SIR GEOFFREY KENDLE
clasps his hands in front of him and
lowers his head, waiting. After a long
time he jerks into life and looks
around, up, down, about him, consults
the palm of his hand.
Still.
He coughs.
Smiles down into the amphitheatre,
points, smiles up at the tower and
says:

I say, that is sweet of Bryan. He's gone
down into the theatre to sit with Dotty
after all,
they're sitting together like friends,
such a shame Dotty doesn't like Bryan
awfully much,
such a shame,
they could be such good friends you
know, they're both insufferable.
I am very disappointed with Penelope, I have
always thought her to be a kind and
generous girl.
You see it shouldn't be left to friends,
Penelope should be down there comforting
her husband in his misery and preventing
him from reading my letters...
He's reading my letters!
Trevor, do you see what Dotty is doing?
Trevor! Stop that man from reading my
letters, they are private and personal
and contain news I do not wish to know!
Very well, very well,
this is going too far, I have said very
little...

He tries to get down again,
the box creaks and wobbles alarmingly,

he scrambles back,
sits on the edge, crouched with anger.

Trevor I warn you, I am about to walk off
this film.

Silence.

Bernie!
Bernie, please go down and prevent that
dreadful man from reading my letters,
you have my permission to be angry,
he always did read other people's letters,
you couldn't leave anything in the
dressing-room without he read it,
his eyes straight to the mirror as soon
as he is brought in...
Trevor, it's no good, with all the will
in the world I cannot concentrate on
whatever I am doing,
whatever it might be, while that man is
reading my mail...
Do you hear?

Silence.
After a pause for decision, SIR GEOFFREY
KENDLE decides.

I withdraw my labour.

He removes his hat and wig.

Be so good as to provide first-class
conveyance to Istanbul,
the Hilton, thence to London, New York or
Languedoc by first-class air, *wagon-lit,*
limousine or state-room...

Putting his leg over, his toe scraping
the side of the box half-heartedly.
Back on the box with both legs, he takes
a position and states:

Starting with a first-class ladder.

The curtain comes down.

While the curtain is down.
FILM. Wide screen and colour with indent
and markings for post-sync,
of SIR GEOFFREY KENDLE trying to get
down from the box,
stopped frame every now and again when
his movements coincide with the content
of the film, the pelt of horses, sepoys
and soldiers, elephant in front projection.
A voice trying hard to fit words to the
mouth of SIR GEOFFREY KENDLE and missing
the cue marks again and again. Desolate howl of
wind, the Cawnpore speech said coldly
and in full, in darkness.

Scene 3

The curtain rises.
Scene: the cavea of the amphitheatre
in the ruins of Priene. Discovered, sitting
in his chair having read letters not
belonging to him, MR LAURENCE D'ORSAY.
The letters in his lap, spectacles with
wire and thread-whipped frames on his
nose. He takes them off. He is grey, balding,
slightly drunk and wearing a bathrobe.
Discovered, also, MR BRYAN DAVID walking
the theatre each row from side to side
and up to the row above sitting in seats
with prominence, the thrones, the royal
box; those seats he might miss on the
way up he is sure of on the way down.
When at the top, later, on reaching the
belt of earth, rubble, scrub, he will

draw his sword and thrust it into the
hot earth, chop at heads of flowers,
scatter debris with the flicking point,
some to enter the collar of MR LAURENCE
D'ORSAY, but not yet. At this moment of
the curtain rising BRYAN DAVID has come
to the first throne, sat in it, stood
up and is walking on, saying:

BRYAN DAVID: Walk on.

MR LAURENCE D'ORSAY: Eh?

BRYAN DAVID: I love that expression to your
  horse, to tell him to walk on.

MR LAURENCE D'ORSAY: Do you talk to him?

BRYAN DAVID: Her.

MR LAURENCE D'ORSAY: Good, always talk to a
  horse.

BRYAN DAVID: Walk on.

MR LAURENCE D'ORSAY: They don't understand a
  word you say. You, you bugger, Bryan. I
  thank God and my housemaster I was taught
  to swim; but not fully clothed, the army
  and the bottle taught me that... tippling
  into canals off bridges.
  It can be dangerous if you swallow the
  water.

BRYAN DAVID: If we had lost you at sea!

MR LAURENCE D'ORSAY: Would have been a story.
  I almost floated off, felt like doing it,
  it was the fact I was hungry drew me to
  your *felucca.* Did you feed us well?

BRYAN DAVID: You said thank you.

MR LAURENCE D'ORSAY: I forget.
How much are you paying for that boat, is
it a *felucca*?

BRYAN DAVID: I'm not sure. My company has
bought it and I'm hiring it from them,
from me, they raised the hire when they
knew I was an actor.

MR LAURENCE D'ORSAY: That is something I
never need worry about.

BRYAN DAVID: I don't know.

MR LAURENCE D'ORSAY: How nice of you to say
so.

BRYAN DAVID: What did I say?

MR LAURENCE D'ORSAY: What are you going to
do after this?

BRYAN DAVID: I don't know.

MR LAURENCE D'ORSAY: You do know. I saw
that greasepot lawyer with you yesterday.

BRYAN DAVID: I don't know that I'll do it.

MR LAURENCE D'ORSAY: Quite right.

BRYAN DAVID: What are you doing?

MR LAURENCE D'ORSAY: Did he come all this
way to talk to you?

BRYAN DAVID: Well, obviously... have you
got anything you want to do Dotty?

MR LAURENCE D'ORSAY: No.
I've got a lot of things I'm going to do but
I don't want to do any of them.
I might do this.

*He holds up the script that came in
the package/envelope, already limp
and splayed where D'ORSAY has flicked
through it with a wet finger.*

BRYAN DAVID: Is it nice?

MR LAURENCE D'ORSAY: I never leave the stage.

BRYAN DAVID: Oh, not a film!

MR LAURENCE D'ORSAY: I've had a bellyful
of films old son. You know that, the way I've
been treated in this one...

BRYAN DAVID: Listen, thank you for the note.

MR LAURENCE D'ORSAY: My dear fellow.
What note?

BRYAN DAVID: About keeping my pecker up.

MR LAURENCE D'ORSAY: You must.

BRYAN DAVID: I didn't understand it.

MR LAURENCE D'ORSAY: Actually I do leave the
stage, but only two or three minutes from
the end and I come back just on the
curtain... not enough time for a quick
one or anything,
hanging about there, worrying.
There's that against taking it on.
In this version as it stands I don't have
another entrance, but I shall insist Alexander
gives me one if I do it... which means
I won't want to do it. I do like to get off
in the first act, don't you?
Ideally?
Anyway, when I come off I like to stay off,
once the sweat gets cold you know... I
shall insist on coming back though in this

play, for the good of the play.
I shan't do it you know... if I have to
come back on two minutes from the end.
See what Geoffrey says. He stays on. A
much bigger part. See what he thinks is
for the best... my confidence is shot to
buggery, Bryan old son.
How are you?

BRYAN DAVID: Oh... you know.

MR LAURENCE D'ORSAY: I feel like getting
myself a nag and tooling off somewhere
till I drop out of the saddle... how do you
feel?

BRYAN DAVID: Great.

MR LAURENCE D'ORSAY: God bless you. Good.

BRYAN DAVID: I'm getting over it now.

MR LAURENCE D'ORSAY: The drink help?

BRYAN DAVID: Yes...

MR LAURENCE D'ORSAY: Bound to.

BRYAN DAVID: ... no, not really.

MR LAURENCE D'ORSAY: Never does.
Listen here, I was very sorry to hear
about your troubles and felt a few words
of consolation privately uttered might help.
You did get the rough end I thought.
Did they?

BRYAN DAVID: Thank you.

MR LAURENCE D'ORSAY: The least I could do.
Penelope's idea. Do you have any chums?

BRYAN DAVID: Yes, of course.

MR LAURENCE D'ORSAY: I thought you might not have any.

BRYAN DAVID: Less and less.

MR LAURENCE D'ORSAY: You can't trust them can you?

BRYAN DAVID: Do you find that?

MR LAURENCE D'ORSAY: My God yes. You, you bugger, you nearly had me drown.
Was that you?

A flick of earth, he
digs it out of his
collar, tries to, stands up and shakes
it down.

BRYAN DAVID: I'm sorry.

MR LAURENCE D'ORSAY: My dear fellow. Watch what you're doing swinging that sword around.

The manner brusque but finishing in a
smile so beautiful, so charming, with such
dazzle as to be totally disarming; the
more so because unexpected.
BRYAN DAVID laughs and salutes with his
sword before returning it.

BRYAN DAVID: Sorry. Dotty, I am sorry.

MR LAURENCE D'ORSAY: Goodness no, no need. What are you doing? Are you walking the house?

BRYAN DAVID: The thing about mates is they can never forgive success... do you find?

MR LAURENCE D'ORSAY: That's a very ordinary thing to say.

You're too young surely. I don't want to
talk about that nonsense, do you?

BRYAN DAVID: No, no.

MR LAURENCE D'ORSAY: Tired of these, these
conversations with such as you;
I like you Bryan, you are an ass and flay
and flounder wearing this hat, that hat,
but you do work... I have never been able
to work do you know?
Geoffrey works until you can't bear him
to pick up a fork,
you want to hold it for him,
what a sharp brain that bumbler has kept.
I'm sure.

BRYAN DAVID: He's a fine actor.

MR LAURENCE D'ORSAY: That's a very ordinary
thing to say.
Again. I don't want to talk about that
nonsense either. Do you?

BRYAN DAVID: His Hamlet the best ever.

MR LAURENCE D'ORSAY: You don't know.
How do you know? You were not born.

BRYAN DAVID: All right love, all right.

BRYAN DAVID annoyed.
The flash smile again from MR LAURENCE
D'ORSAY and a wave of his hand.

MR LAURENCE D'ORSAY: I don't mean to be
rude to you Bryan.
I don't old son.
Listen here, can we get to know each other
do you think? If we ferret each other out
do you know... I would like that, you?

BRYAN DAVID: Have we the time?

MR LAURENCE D'ORSAY: Half an hour for you
and two, three days for me.
You can't have much.

BRYAN DAVID: Cold? Won't there be the
inevitable settling into first lies,
second lies, truth?

MR LAURENCE D'ORSAY: Not the way it goes
old son, first lies, second lies, truth
and then more lies similar to the first.
But do lie, they're most important. I like
lies immoderately.
Told.

BRYAN DAVID: Today's gone already. Tomorrow
will see you off.

MR LAURENCE D'ORSAY: My bags packed?
Sent packing?
Might. Might take a boat home so we can
talk, not your *felucca*... a funnel job
with facilities for inside walkee, can do?
I would like to know you better Bryan.
Did you have an education?

BRYAN DAVID: You know me well enough.

MR LAURENCE D'ORSAY: Few people need more
then a smattering.
Those rows of empty seats get played to
don't they? I shall sit down before I
drum the shades, get given the Greek bird.
You watch when Geoffrey enters,
how he itches,
can't sit, lurches into thunder one shoulder
low soon as he sniffs a cue,
he can't hear 'em,

didn't you know that, he's deaf all down
one side, surely you knew?
Thought you young men watched.
Look, the sky is magnificent. Can't you look
at it?

BRYAN DAVID: Isn't it dull? Just blue.

MR LAURENCE D'ORSAY: Now I know you, did
you go to RADA? Scholarship from St Dunstans?
Blind as a bat.
What with you blind and me dumb and Sir deaf
all down one side, what heroes!

BRYAN DAVID: But don't you get tired of it
blue every day?

MR LAURENCE D'ORSAY: I'm tired of everything
old lad, it's a condition.
I am grateful to you for walking off the
picture, have you spoken to the newspapers?

BRYAN DAVID: Which side?

MR LAURENCE D'ORSAY: That friend of yours
from *Look Magazine*, have you spoken to him?

BRYAN DAVID: I didn't do it for you Dotty.
I walked off for the good of the film,
because I felt that what I was being
asked to do was wrong.

MR LAURENCE D'ORSAY: Talk to them at once
and say that. Do you know where they are?
That is a worthwhile thing to say and
irreproachable. I shall say nothing do you
see, I shall merely nod my head.
They were clicking around the elephant
earlier on, were you there?
No, I thought that very odd. They were

clicking like mad so I knew you were there,
but you say you weren't? Would they be
interested in photographs of Geoffrey, he
was there?
His off side. Don't ever get off hind of
him on the stage.
He won't let you. But you ought to wire
the *Daily Mail* I think, they always come
up with the puffs reliably... it can't
be easy for them when there is so much
happening in the world,
stage-struck or cunt-struck, I don't know
what... eh!

*A roar of laughter from MR LAURENCE
D'ORSAY and then silence. He asks:*

Do they serve you well?

BRYAN DAVID: Trevor is hoping you will
say nothing...

MR LAURENCE D'ORSAY: Old son, old son, I
am dumb, Geoffrey deaf down the one side,
you blind...
To some things.
D'ailleurs old lad I am dumb by contract,
dum bene se gesserit, or
so long as he keeps his nose clean,
my contract is a masterpiece of Hollywood
habeas corpus cum clausa,
lawyers read my morality clauses and
masturbate, I am banned from entering
the legal life of four countries,
*clausulae inconsuetae semper inducant
suspicionem...* mine excite sequacity,
my last fully signed and sealed made the
Index, are you a Catholic?

I shall say nothing for fear of *felo de se*,
professionally...
I hope Geoffrey
has managed to persuade the boy-wonder I
should be kept on.
I need the life old son, money no
but I do need the life. Look, we fight tooth
and claw but we both need the life...
I need the work, or rather the proximity
of the work... you're not blind to beauty
though are you,
not when it has tits hung on it old son?
We'll give them dinner tonight,
that fellow from *Look Magazine* and his girl
friend. Let me give them dinner. Then you
materialize having walked off the film and
give your reasons, then I say nothing
and shake hands, 'goodbye we are leaving the
day after tomorrow'. That way we all stay
clean and only you are sued.

BRYAN DAVID: I only walked off the set Dotty.

MR LAURENCE D'ORSAY: Same thing.

BRYAN DAVID: No. I expect to be asked back.

MR LAURENCE D'ORSAY: So do I old love. But
should I not be do you see...
Do you mind if I sit down?

BRYAN DAVID: Why should I?

MR LAURENCE D'ORSAY: Thought you were
entitled to the courtesy, only my neck aches
to talk to you up there, join me.

BRYAN DAVID: No.

MR LAURENCE D'ORSAY: My dear fellow, you must
please yourself.

Surely you will not eat humble pie and go
back after the way you have been treated,
no, you wouldn't, Bryan? No film is
worth it believe me, I know, I've been on
them all...

BRYAN DAVID: Loyalty might make me reconsider,
isn't it important?

MR LAURENCE D'ORSAY: Look here, you had better
not rely on *Look Magazine*, when does it
appear, once a month or weekly? No, you need
a fistful of dailies at once.
Shouldn't be difficult.
We'll set to on the telephone as soon as
we get back to the hotel. I'm waiting on
Penelope or I'd ring some chums now.
She came out today but I've seen very
little of her as you can imagine.

BRYAN DAVID: You're the only one though.

MR LAURENCE D'ORSAY: We're tottering. What did you
say?

BRYAN DAVID: Nothing, nothing.

MR LAURENCE D'ORSAY: But then we always have been.
Nothing new there. My wife, my beautiful young
wife. What she'll do... You on
your own again tonight? You might
like to give Penelope dinner yourself
my flower? Please... I mean we're tottering
and she'll shoot off very soon if she hasn't
done so already... feel free.
But I don't need to tell you that. It's all
come to a head because she won't have any
children do you know.

BRYAN DAVID: I'm sorry.

MR LAURENCE D'ORSAY: It was silly of me to
mention it, but I did, I got to think I
would like some.
She isn't frantic about them as some
people are, I mean children sit with her
happily on the occasions they are brought
together. I know she is liked by them
for being calm and kind and not buzzing.
I know that from my eldest son's children.
So it must be she doesn't want to have my
children.

BRYAN DAVID: Do you actually want...

MR LAURENCE D'ORSAY: Don't you?

BRYAN DAVID: Yes I do... I've got, I've
had children...

MR LAURENCE D'ORSAY: I've always wanted kids.

BRYAN DAVID: But, I mean is it likely?

MR LAURENCE D'ORSAY: I beg your pardon?

BRYAN DAVID: Nothing... you said your son?

MR LAURENCE D'ORSAY: No no.
You don't know about children, don't regard
them as children unless you do things with
them like all the things you may do with
children. I realised some small time ago
that although I had sired two, three sons
and a daughter I had never had any
children. Does that sound nonsense to you
old son? No, of course it don't because
you are a sensitive chap, you see I've always
been well-off, money and the rest, I was
never poor even when young.
I don't think I'm being romantic when I

say that being poor along the side of
your children means you know what it is
to have children,
living in the same rooms do you see?
I would have liked that and thought it not
too late but Penelope wouldn't hear of it.
She says she can't have 'em. That is a
lie, but I allow it;
look at the arse on her, she can have
any amount of children that cradle in
her haunches... do you know.
I hope I'm not verging on the indelicate,
my tulip, discussing Penelope's twat...

BRYAN DAVID: It's not something she keeps
to herself.

MR LAURENCE D'ORSAY: I beg your pardon?

BRYAN DAVID: Is it though?

MR LAURENCE D'ORSAY: How very nice of you
to say so.
Anyway, feel free. She finds you a bit of
a mountebank as we all do, but I think
she's quite fond of you.
If I live to be eighty I could have
fifteen years of children, my word,
little bastards.

BRYAN DAVID: You've got grandchildren.

MR LAURENCE D'ORSAY: Some, most of them
grown up and in jail, transit or expensive
sanatoria being flushed out or stood up.
There are three little brats I'm taken
with, still below my knee,
my eldest son's brats,
he won't let me near them without I bring

Penelope... quite right. No, I am set on my
own you know.
Tell me about yours?

BRYAN DAVID: No.

MR LAURENCE D'ORSAY: I'm delighted to hear it.
Do you see them often? Balls are the things
they love balls, any child will thank you
for a ball.
You know what she'll do don't you, eh?
She'll piss off and have some by something
nasty blow by blow in *Look Magazine*.

Another flick of earth,
MR LAURENCE D'ORSAY shoots his hand
up to his neck and turns it to reproach
BRYAN DAVID who is sitting very low
down and not responsible.

That wasn't you?

BRYAN DAVID: No. Look I'm interested, are
you still capable of having children?

MR LAURENCE D'ORSAY: Never was, squire. I
leave that to the women.

BRYAN DAVID: You know what I mean.

MR LAURENCE D'ORSAY: Who was it then? I'm
not going to be made a figure of fun and
have spitballs flicked at me...

A slither of earth from the hill
above the amphitheatre, some stones
and a shout. MR LAURENCE D'ORSAY
stands up to look and almost at once
sits down again, smiles and offers
the chair alongside to BRYAN DAVID.

Geoffrey, before Geoffrey joins us why
don't you have this chair and tell me
what you think...

BRYAN DAVID: No. I don't want a chair.

MR LAURENCE D'ORSAY: We have Trevor by the
short hairs you know – you walking off as
well as... me... puts me in a much
better position do you see.
What do you think? I value your opinion
dear heart.

BRYAN DAVID: Go home.

MR LAURENCE D'ORSAY: But not very highly.

BRYAN DAVID: You don't need the money.

MR LAURENCE D'ORSAY: Hark old son, I get
paid not to work.

BRYAN DAVID: Yes, so... ?

MR LAURENCE D'ORSAY: Have I told you how
I got this film?

BRYAN DAVID: Yes.

MR LAURENCE D'ORSAY: Which version do you
know?

BRYAN DAVID: The version you told me.

MR LAURENCE D'ORSAY: I doubt if it's the
true version.

BRYAN DAVID: Never mind, I still think you
should go home.

MR LAURENCE D'ORSAY: Thank you.

BRYAN DAVID: Don't you? I mean if you don't
care about the money, don't you think you
should? What do you want to do?

MR LAURENCE D'ORSAY: Not much.
>   Stay here and do the work
>   and watch my young wife, she'll
>   go if I go... she might, and
>   if she goes it all goes... the
>   work, soldiers and horses and
>   young women who find it exciting...
>   Have you seen any rushes?
>
>   *BRYAN DAVID nods his head, looks up*
>   *the hill from where there is another*
>   *small slither of stones.*
>
>   You're very brave, or very foolish and I
>   don't know which – apparently she is very good
>   would you say? And me?

BRYAN DAVID: I think Sir Geoffrey needs help.

MR LAURENCE D'ORSAY: Everybody seems to
>   think so. I would like that, if she was, you know
>   when you're doing good work don't you?
>   Like you, old lad, I want to finish it in
>   spite of the director's nonsense.
>   I have to face relatives when I go home,
>   you see I know the present Canning. Lord
>   Canning, he still feels responsible for India,
>   and so he should.
>   More than that, I want to stay in this
>   fascinating country in the company of
>   pros and horses do you know, soldiers
>   and horses... where else, talking to pleasant
>   young men like you, the company of friends, soldiers
>   and actors and horses. Why not?

BRYAN DAVID: It's favourite.

MR LAURENCE D'ORSAY: It is. I haven't heard
>   that expression for years. You have a gift
>   for that sort of thing, do you write? Do

> you mind if I make a note of that... I do
> like to take down any odd phrases, a
> useful practise... do you write?

BRYAN DAVID: It's finding the time.

MR LAURENCE D'ORSAY: Isn't it?
> You will old son. Have you a pencil, I
> have the back of an old envelope here,
> I am without *my* notebook...
> Then again you say go home,
> a ticklish problem there at the present
> time as you will imagine,
> where to go – in the event of losing a
> wife you do invariably find yourself
> without a house to go to... they change
> the locks, first thing they do.

BRYAN DAVID: Stay just where you are Sir
> Geoffrey, don't move.

> *A slither of stones,*
> *BRYAN DAVID goes up the stone seats*
> *of the amphitheatre to help SIR GEOFFREY*
> *KENDLE. As he goes there is another*
> *slither of stone and earth and SIR*
> *GEOFFREY arrives on his backside in a rush.*
> *Enter SIR GEOFFREY KENDLE bringing*
> *himself down in his seat. He passes*
> *BRYAN DAVID on the way.*

MR LAURENCE D'ORSAY: Ah there you are
> Geoffrey, any news?

SIR GEOFFREY KENDLE: Where is everybody?
> Will you let me get my breath back... I
> came down there...

BRYAN DAVID: Are you all right?

SIR GEOFFREY KENDLE: Shall I tell you in a
> moment?

MR LAURENCE D'ORSAY: It's good of you to
    have listened Bryan old love, I hope I
    haven't bored the pants off you.
    I am grateful.
    Bryan has walked off the set Geoffrey.

SIR GEOFFREY KENDLE: Yes. So have I, to
    some extent.
    Actually I fell off it.

MR LAURENCE D'ORSAY: Thank you Bryan.

He gets out of his chair and taps
BRYAN DAVID lightly on his arm,
smiles and walks back to sit down
again. After a pause, while BRYAN
stands over SIR GEOFFREY with his
hand on the old man's shoulder,
D'ORSAY says:

You'll want to know Geoffrey, in the papers,
    Carole is dead yesterday.

SIR GEOFFREY KENDLE: Is she?

MR LAURENCE D'ORSAY: Do you want the
    telegram given you?

SIR GEOFFREY KENDLE: I don't know what to
    say.

MR LAURENCE D'ORSAY: I thought I'd tell you
    straight away.

SIR GEOFFREY KENDLE: Oh please, thank you.
    Did you see her before we came out?

MR LAURENCE D'ORSAY: I never liked her.
    I did see her, she was very sweet.

SIR GEOFFREY KENDLE: She never liked you.

MR LAURENCE D'ORSAY: She was very sweet to
Penelope which surprised me. Went out of her
way to be sweet.

SIR GEOFFREY KENDLE: How very sweet.

MR LAURENCE D'ORSAY: Yes wasn't it? I was
astonished, had hoped to thank her somehow.
I was touched.

SIR GEOFFREY KENDLE: That's awfully kind
of you Dotty.

MR LAURENCE D'ORSAY: Will I keep the
telegram for you?

SIR GEOFFREY KENDLE: Do, please. Does it say
when?

MR LAURENCE D'ORSAY: There's just the
briefest report in the paper. I expect the
telegram tells you but I saw what it was
and didn't read any more, wanting you to
when you felt you could,
you may get more out of it than I did.

SIR GEOFFREY KENDLE: You make it impossible
for me to be angry with you.

MR LAURENCE D'ORSAY: Why should you be?

SIR GEOFFREY KENDLE: Well, you know what
you're like.

MR LAURENCE D'ORSAY: Bit late in the day
chum.

SIR GEOFFREY KENDLE: Was there anything else?

MR LAURENCE D'ORSAY: Some things you ought
to know but they can wait.

SIR GEOFFREY KENDLE: Will she be buried do
you think, she didn't want to be... I

suppose that ghastly man with the gold-
rimmed spectacles will want to bury her,
gold teeth,
did you ever meet him? I did, he was
always there.

MR LAURENCE D'ORSAY: What was he?

SIR GEOFFREY KENDLE: From round here I gathered
when he wasn't in London.

MR LAURENCE D'ORSAY: Boy friend?

SIR GEOFFREY KENDLE: Yes they've been married
for years, we were all against it at the time
which made her all the more determined, poor
dear. Anything else?

MR LAURENCE D'ORSAY: It will keep.

SIR GEOFFREY KENDLE: He was called Vincenzo
so perhaps he wasn't from round here. Do
you think I should write to him?

MR LAURENCE D'ORSAY: What would you say?

SIR GEOFFREY KENDLE: How sorry.
How sorry I am.

MR LAURENCE D'ORSAY: You are.

SIR GEOFFREY KENDLE: Yes I know.

MR LAURENCE D'ORSAY: She's always been the
one person to you.

SIR GEOFFREY KENDLE: Yes I know.

MR LAURENCE D'ORSAY: You were like brother
and sister, or more than that more than
that – they fight so usually and are not
close... you were like David and Jonathan.

SIR GEOFFREY KENDLE: Yes, I know. Were we?
Did you know her father? I didn't but he

probably disliked me.
Gosh that was ages ago.
You were the one then, everybody liked you.
I can't imagine why.
I thought I'd just tell him how sorry I
was.

MR LAURENCE D'ORSAY: But you can't you see
because you are. He'll have hundreds of
letters won't he and you'll only join...

SIR GEOFFREY KENDLE: I wonder should I go?

MR LAURENCE D'ORSAY: What can you do?

SIR GEOFFREY KENDLE: Yes I know. I'm wondering
if Trevor will let me go... I don't see how
he can...

MR LAURENCE D'ORSAY: Did you speak to him?

SIR GEOFFREY KENDLE: Yes I did.

MR LAURENCE D'ORSAY: Bryan has a tale to tell
don't you Bryan?

BRYAN DAVID: Heave on my hand Sir Geoffrey.

*He sticks out his hand to help SIR
GEOFFREY KENDLE to his feet. SIR GEOFFREY
dusts his seat absently, thanks BRYAN
with a pat and asks him:*

SIR GEOFFREY KENDLE: Did you know Carole?

BRYAN DAVID: No.

MR LAURENCE D'ORSAY: No, about himself.

BRYAN DAVID: Carole who?

SIR GEOFFREY KENDLE: I only asked you
because she was always involving herself
with the avant-garde,

buying vans for people – it rarely came
to anything... you didn't know her?

BRYAN DAVID: No.

SIR GEOFFREY KENDLE: She's an old friend.

BRYAN DAVID: I'm sorry.

MR LAURENCE D'ORSAY: I shouldn't say anything
Geoffrey.

SIR GEOFFREY KENDLE: Does it say what she
did?

MR LAURENCE D'ORSAY: Not a word.

SIR GEOFFREY KENDLE: Good good and after
all she may not have done.

BRYAN DAVID: I would like to say more
than just sorry, but perhaps I should
just leave you alone.

SIR GEOFFREY KENDLE: How very kind of you
Bryan, would you?

BRYAN DAVID: Yes, I'll go and find Penelope.

MR LAURENCE D'ORSAY: Would you Bryan?

SIR GEOFFREY KENDLE: I would like to talk
to you Bryan because I've been thinking
about you... but if you don't mind me
saying so marriage may not be the answer.
Bryan is getting married Dotty.
No, I'm wrong, he was getting married
but it's off – didn't she end up in a hotel
with some very famous actor,
older than you Dotty,
wasn't that it? An old friend... let me
speak to you as one who has been married
once in his lifetime. I do know that if

you're worried about whether or not you're
capable or not or whether you are or you
aren't you won't find out by being married
and dragging some poor girl into it.
Look at me, I haven't the faintest
idea what I am!
I could always manage to do it I think
quite well with the minimum fraughtage,
I wasn't formidable,
my place on the bill I could certainly
be followed and often was,
no doubt topped... you had better ask
my friends about that,
they'll all have their own way of looking
at me. She's terribly grand now, a very
wealthy family,
isn't that a coincidence... don't I
know your wife, didn't she come into my
room one night with Yale across her chest,
of course, you're wearing it,
my wife was American, I said poor
girl have a towel and she mentioned you,
isn't Hollywood such a waste,
all those swimming pools? That's how I
lost my wife,
did you know, have I told you? Well you
see I don't as you know, otherwise I would
have been out to your boat... but she
assumed I did and dived in with all her
friends calling things quite jolly
but hurtful,
you see I was the new English husband.
What could I do? I was obviously expected
to enter the water if you please. I went
up to my room, my luggage, and donned it.
Down to here... they were for English
people, striped down to here. But you see

these dear Americans were half-naked
swimming about like the Tarzans they
resembled and eventually tested for;
a rubber cap,
we all wore them, and these perfectly
respectable long things... I found the
ladder and entered the water, prepared to
do it, teetering a little at the edge of
it, new husband you see,
they laughed. How they laughed. You know
how they can laugh when they are American,
rich, educated beyond their means and they
don't need you this time around?
I never saw her again. I got out dripping
and packed. I hear she's terribly grand
now, I hear she goes to the theatre now,
another thing they've started doing a lot,
mind you they always did,
they called it something else. She wrote
asking me for my autograph quite recently,
so she does talk about me to her friends.
Is that any help to you at all? Bryan?
Bryan is worried about is he queer, Dotty.

MR LAURENCE D'ORSAY: Is he?

SIR GEOFFREY KENDLE: He thinks not.

MR LAURENCE D'ORSAY: Does he want to talk
about it?

SIR GEOFFREY KENDLE: Do you Bryan? Bryan?

BRYAN DAVID laughs, up on the stone
seats and swinging his sword,
flicking earth down into the cavea
of the amphitheatre.

BRYAN DAVID: Look, I'll go and look for
Penelope.

SIR GEOFFREY KENDLE: Are you throwing
   things? I fell off that box Bryan, you
   were right to distrust it.
   Shall we eat tonight?

MR LAURENCE D'ORSAY: We're all eating tonight.

SIR GEOFFREY KENDLE: How kind of you Dotty,
   did you arrange it?

BRYAN DAVID: Good, great. I am sorry.

MR LAURENCE D'ORSAY: Now keep away from
   directors. We must stick together.

BRYAN DAVID: Yes, all right. Sir Geoffrey?

SIR GEOFFREY KENDLE: Bryan.

BRYAN DAVID: You're not deaf.

SIR GEOFFREY KENDLE: No no, not in the least.

BRYAN DAVID: No, I thought not.
   Your friend is a liar.

   *Another laugh and exit BRYAN DAVID.
   The two old gentlemen sitting in their
   chairs. Silent a while, then:*

SIR GEOFFREY KENDLE: Funny boy.

MR LAURENCE D'ORSAY: He's not bent, Penelope
   would have told me.

SIR GEOFFREY KENDLE: Is she still talking
   to you?

MR LAURENCE D'ORSAY: Barely.

SIR GEOFFREY KENDLE: I want desperately to
   go back to my hotel and shut myself in my
   room.

MR LAURENCE D'ORSAY: My love.

SIR GEOFFREY KENDLE: I shall never forgive
    Trevor for leaving me alone on that box,
    alone Dotty,
    you know how I hate being alone,
    they're all gone you know. I was left alone.

MR LAURENCE D'ORSAY: Who?

SIR GEOFFREY KENDLE: Oh everybody, everybody,
    all skedaddled and left me on a box like a
    statue on Trafalgar Square...
    I made the gesture, I walked off, a thing
    I've never done before...

MR LAURENCE D'ORSAY: I have mate.

SIR GEOFFREY KENDLE: Yes, yes, you have. I
    have never done such a thing before,
    no matter what. An empty gesture it turns
    out because there is no sign of them
    where they should be, not anywhere, not up
    the tower, not in their lorries, not sight
    nor sound,
    how Bernie can vanish without a trace is
    beyond me. There must be a trace of Bernie
    but I didn't find it.
    Gone.

MR LAURENCE D'ORSAY: Are you saying that?

SIR GEOFFREY KENDLE: I am and I'm not fuzzy.
    I looked. Fell off that box and there you
    are... *Mary Rose.*

MR LAURENCE D'ORSAY: Don't be silly.

Silence. They both of them sit
in silence and listen.
After a while SIR GEOFFREY KENDLE
puts out a hand on MR LAURENCE D'ORSAY's
knee and continues:

SIR GEOFFREY KENDLE: I'm not being silly.
I looked. Then I came down to you, fell
down here. There was a moment in limbo
with a bush when I thought you had gone
also, but something gave and here we are.
I believe they have walked out on us.

MR LAURENCE D'ORSAY: Did you drop off or
anything?

SIR GEOFFREY KENDLE: I closed my eyes
to compose myself as I do, once or twice,
said a difficult speech as I do, once or
twice...

MR LAURENCE D'ORSAY: Gone off somewhere.

SIR GEOFFREY KENDLE: Certainly gone off
somewhere, where?

MR LAURENCE D'ORSAY: Not even a Turk?

SIR GEOFFREY KENDLE: Not even. So I came down.

MR LAURENCE D'ORSAY: Did you look in that
gin palace where they skulk?

SIR GEOFFREY KENDLE: Gin palace?

MR LAURENCE D'ORSAY: We call them gin palaces in
the desert. Oh.

A great sigh of nostalgia for the desert.

SIR GEOFFREY KENDLE: Oh I wouldn't know; the
big lorry goes up and down?

MR LAURENCE D'ORSAY: Yes.

SIR GEOFFREY KENDLE: No.

MR LAURENCE D'ORSAY: Did you not look?

SIR GEOFFREY KENDLE: Yes I did, the first

place I looked. No. Should we have let
Bryan go?

MR LAURENCE D'ORSAY: Why not?

SIR GEOFFREY KENDLE: Suppose he's never
seen again?

MR LAURENCE D'ORSAY: Do him the world of
good, professionally.

*SIR GEOFFREY KENDLE picks up the
script in its envelope/package and
addressed to him. He takes it out
and cracks it open, asks:*

SIR GEOFFREY KENDLE: Have you looked at
this?

MR LAURENCE D'ORSAY: I've read it.

SIR GEOFFREY KENDLE: I've had it before.

*He shows MR LAURENCE D'ORSAY the tiny
pencil marks on the title page.*

MR LAURENCE D'ORSAY: What do you say?

SIR GEOFFREY KENDLE: Is it anywhere near
good?

MR LAURENCE D'ORSAY: Have you not read it
yet?

SIR GEOFFREY KENDLE: Should I?

MR LAURENCE D'ORSAY: It's worth a look.

SIR GEOFFREY KENDLE: Two main characters I see.

MR LAURENCE D'ORSAY: Read it.

SIR GEOFFREY KENDLE: Listen.
Can you hear anything? No birds, the crickets

stopped and isn't it nice? Penelope's
eagle stood still in the sky, slip.

MR LAURENCE D'ORSAY: Is it before or after
earthquakes that you don't hear birds, they
stop their twittering?

SIR GEOFFREY KENDLE: Before.

MR LAURENCE D'ORSAY: Are you sure? Those
bloody great stones of the temple must
have toppled somehow... I suspect we're
on an earthquake belt.

SIR GEOFFREY KENDLE: Before.

MR LAURENCE D'ORSAY: No, after.

SIR GEOFFREY KENDLE: Dotty it must be before
because we haven't had one have we?

MR LAURENCE D'ORSAY: Listen, page seventeen
I like... page seventeen.
Will you read Traille?

SIR GEOFFREY KENDLE: Who?

MR LAURENCE D'ORSAY: Traille, there. 'I have
locked my evacuee child in the linen cupboard.'

He points to the line in the script,
as he says it,
SIR GEOFFREY KENDLE peers at page
seventeen, finds it and says:

SIR GEOFFREY KENDLE: 'I have locked my evacuee
child in the linen cupboard.'

MR LAURENCE D'ORSAY: 'You know best old man,
but you risk nits in your linen.'

SIR GEOFFREY KENDLE: Do you want me to go
on?

*MR LAURENCE D'ORSAY nods. SIR GEOFFREY
KENDLE continues, reading very badly.*

SIR GEOFFREY KENDLE: 'It's better that
   than the sight of him trouserless, jam
   on his sparrow face, the one hand
   reaching far up his nose, the other
   searching for crumbs in the fold of his
   tiny foreskin at breakfast...'
   I don't think I want to do this.

MR LAURENCE D'ORSAY: 'Traille old chap,
   are you anything like Jewish?'

SIR GEOFFREY KENDLE: 'Not any more, I
   used to be before the war...'
   Do you?

MR LAURENCE D'ORSAY: 'Then you will be able
   to get petrol?'

SIR GEOFFREY KENDLE: 'I am not able to.'

MR LAURENCE D'ORSAY: 'Your friends are all
   over here now. Most of them have greengrocery
   shops in Leeds. Very few of you will leave
   now you are come. I'm not asking you to. No.'

SIR GEOFFREY KENDLE: 'And you are not likely
   to because...'

MR LAURENCE D'ORSAY: 'Because I am a person
   has a great deal of time for...'

SIR GEOFFREY KENDLE: '... because you owe
   me money.'
   I can't think why Alexander sent me this.
   Do you want to do it?

MR LAURENCE D'ORSAY: I don't know. Do you?

SIR GEOFFREY KENDLE: What is it, two
   characters, two old men on a beach somewhere

during the war.
I don't think we want to do that do we?

MR LAURENCE D'ORSAY: Perhaps not.

But he does, very much.

SIR GEOFFREY KENDLE: I mean there doesn't
seem to be anything there, do we develop
as people do you think? I can't see us
being anywhere more than two old men in
deckchairs can you?
What will you do?
I'll do 'gone away, not known at this address'
I'm afraid... see here, I've had this twice
already. I wish you hadn't asked me to read
it, I don't want it again...

MR LAURENCE D'ORSAY: I thought there might
be something in it for us.

SIR GEOFFREY KENDLE: Goodness me no. You
didn't!

MR LAURENCE D'ORSAY: I thought we might do
it next.

SIR GEOFFREY KENDLE: You hate long runs.

MR LAURENCE D'ORSAY: I thought this was
pretty certain not to have a long run.

SIR GEOFFREY KENDLE: If we do it we are
certain to give it a long run.

MR LAURENCE D'ORSAY: I do dreadful things
if I'm bored.
Better not do it then. Are you sure?

SIR GEOFFREY KENDLE: Yes I am, they'll
love it if we do it.

MR LAURENCE D'ORSAY: I mean you'll want
   work now... will you?

SIR GEOFFREY KENDLE: Why?

MR LAURENCE D'ORSAY: I was buttering up
   Bryan, I know he's got something. Did you
   see them at the hotel, I pointed them out
   to you. That greasepot lawyer come to talk.
   They swam into the middle of the pool to
   talk to be in private,
   and Penelope swam between their legs to listen.

SIR GEOFFREY KENDLE: What did she hear?

MR LAURENCE D'ORSAY: Nothing, they closed up.

SIR GEOFFREY KENDLE: I've got far too
   much to do, things I can't ever hope to
   finish... I'm very worried about the way
   we've been left...
   Where do you think everybody has gone?

MR LAURENCE D'ORSAY: Will you patch it up
   or have you really walked off?

SIR GEOFFREY KENDLE: I hope I'll patch it
   up. I hope they'll apologize, I mean where
   would I go?

MR LAURENCE D'ORSAY: Andrew is at 'The Briars'
   with his friends so there won't be room for
   you there.

SIR GEOFFREY KENDLE: I don't want to go
   to Eaton Square.

MR LAURENCE D'ORSAY: You can't, the place
   is stripped.

SIR GEOFFREY KENDLE: No, that's in the
   country. They took everything.

MR LAURENCE D'ORSAY: Then they did Eaton Square.

SIR GEOFFREY KENDLE: Did they? Oh dear, I thought disaster this morning... I can't go to New York because of Americans and you know what's happening in Languedoc don't you?

MR LAURENCE D'ORSAY: No.

SIR GEOFFREY KENDLE: Hasn't anybody written to me from Languedoc?

MR LAURENCE D'ORSAY: I don't think so.

SIR GEOFFREY KENDLE: Well, you know who's there don't you? I can't go there. I can't go anywhere. I do wish friends would not take invitations so literally leaving me nowhere to live. Where will you go if you go?

MR LAURENCE D'ORSAY: Is it certain?

SIR GEOFFREY KENDLE: I'm sorry Dotty, you have gone too far this time. I can't understand why you do it married to Penelope who is surely enough... I mean do you still manage... ? Er... ?

MR LAURENCE D'ORSAY: Yes. I'm still a man.

SIR GEOFFREY KENDLE: My God, how desperately sad.

A long pause. SIR GEOFFREY KENDLE searches for his sun cream.

MR LAURENCE D'ORSAY: Is there no chance he will change his mind?

SIR GEOFFREY KENDLE: I doubt it.

MR LAURENCE D'ORSAY: Suppose something like
I am nominated for an Oscar?

SIR GEOFFREY KENDLE: We would all be very
happy.

MR LAURENCE D'ORSAY: Well I am, for *Windows*.

SIR GEOFFREY KENDLE: Did you do that?

MR LAURENCE D'ORSAY: Some of it.

SIR GEOFFREY KENDLE: Why?

MR LAURENCE D'ORSAY: I was thrown off that
version of *The Tempest*.

SIR GEOFFREY KENDLE: Oh Dotty I'm so pleased
for you – is it absolutely marvellous?

MR LAURENCE D'ORSAY: *The Tempest?*

SIR GEOFFREY KENDLE: Were you in that? I
Hear it's absolutely marvellous.

MR LAURENCE D'ORSAY: *Windows*.

SIR GEOFFREY KENDLE: How splendid, is it
very very good?

MR LAURENCE D'ORSAY: I'm told it seems to
fit.

SIR GEOFFREY KENDLE: How marvellous!

MR LAURENCE D'ORSAY: So, shall I tell him
I'm nominated for this Oscar?

SIR GEOFFREY KENDLE: He'll know, love.

MR LAURENCE D'ORSAY: Shall I tell him I am?

SIR GEOFFREY KENDLE: Have you been before?

MR LAURENCE D'ORSAY: I don't think so.

SIR GEOFFREY KENDLE: How marvellous.

MR LAURENCE D'ORSAY: There's no chance he'll
change his mind?

SIR GEOFFREY KENDLE: I don't think so, Trevor
has a strange integrity, he's a bit like you.

MR LAURENCE D'ORSAY: Then I shan't tell him.

SIR GEOFFREY KENDLE: You'd have to find him
first. If you can find him... Not even a
patch of grease where Bernie had been.
Look at that, a tortoise, what's that on
its back, written?
Do you see?

*A tortoise moves slightly in the heat
between the chairs. The two old
gentlemen watch it for a while.
MR LAURENCE D'ORSAY reaches out a
finger and twirls the tortoise to see
what is written on its shell.*

MR LAURENCE D'ORSAY: It's marked 'SPARKS'.

SIR GEOFFREY KENDLE: Turkish? I know they
have a Woolworths, do they?

MR LAURENCE D'ORSAY: Here, here Sparks!

SIR GEOFFREY KENDLE: He belongs to
electrics, sparks, he belongs to them.
Now you've lost his head.
To be marked 'SPARKS'! Will it come off in
the rain do you think? They live for years
you know. Just imagine years from now to be
roaming the hills still marked 'SPARKS',
'PROPS', 'WARDROBE'.
That's a good name for a tortoise isn't it,
when you look at it? Wardrobe?

The Hairdressers have one with 'HARE'
written on its back, as in jugged – quite
unconscious humour, they're Swedish... and
they can't spell,
awfully well,
I can't help thinking how appropriately
'HARE' might have been dropped on the bald
pate of poor serious Aeschylus,
oh what a fate for a tragic writer – how
unfair.
Dotty, I do hope they haven't gone off
and left us to fend,
because I really don't have anywhere to
go where I won't be a nuisance... and if
you and Penelope are... are you?
Do you know what 'hair in the gate' means?
It means they have to do it again for a
little bit of hair wiggling in the gate
of the camera, I didn't know cameras
had gates did you?
I was sure it was a compliment.

MR LAURENCE D'ORSAY: It is upsetting, this
poor tortoise marked for life?

SIR GEOFFREY KENDLE: I think so. Don't you?
And all these plastic cups in every ditch,
behind every wall,
they won't ever rot or anything, years
from now... if we're the only ones left
still here, should we not clear them up?

MR LAURENCE D'ORSAY: No.

He tosses the plastic cup he is
holding to join the others.
The curtain comes down.

THE END

ACROSS FROM THE GARDEN OF ALLAH

Characters

BARBARA

DOUGLAS

BELLHOP

None of the other characters described are seen though they are there. As CYNTHIA would say, the space around them is felt.

ACROSS FROM THE GARDEN OF ALLAH received its first West End performance at the Comedy Theatre (preceded by a short tour) on 28th February 1986, with the following cast:

BARBARA, Glenda Jackson
DOUGLAS, Nigel Hawthorne
BELLHOP, Andy Lucas

DIRECTION: Ron Daniels
DESIGN: Ralph Koltai
LIGHTING: David Hersey

ACT ONE

Sunset Boulevard. 1982.

The curtain rises. Enter BARBARA.

BARBARA: Enter Barbara, hot, tired, faded English
    beauty type,
    wonderful, this is it!
    Hollywood, Sunset Boulevard, this is it,
    my first time ever,
    flushed nervous excited with husband, screenwriter
    English screenwriter, makes a difference he says
    paid less, writes more, hopes to live longer;
    won't though he says if he has to keep coming
    to Hollywood,
    will,
    well, might because I have decided to keep
    coming with him to see he does live
    longer, or be with him when he goes;
    the right food, that sort of thing,
    it's wonderful though, look at it! All those
    hoardings, all those films, all those
    names, some of them names of people we know,
    I know, because Douglas, that's my husband,
    can never remember names, especially names,
    who have been in films he has written, he's
    drunk at the moment. He always is drunk
    when he flies he says, he can only fly when
    he's drunk he says and I think he means it,
    poor Douglas.

    Of course it's drugs here, drink is out he says
    drunks are not tolerated in Hollywood, you
    can do anything else but you must not be
    known as a drunk,

even if you're a screenwriter, don't times
change? because you won't deliver, he says,
and you've got to deliver no matter what,
well he won't deliver, not for hours yet I
shouldn't think... he
hates swimming.

Listen, can you hear it? The pool? We've done
three hotels in
the past hour, he couldn't work in the first
two, one was the
Beverly Wilshire,
I loved it,
he hated it,
Home Counties hacienda, he says he can never
work in the Beverly
Wilshire, I wouldn't know. The other was a
concrete bunker,
tiny pool, spewed on carpets,
slabs of timber texture gloom, the tiny cold
shadowed pool
full of men who all
stopped whatever they were doing, leap frogging
or whatever
and LOOKED at me!
which won't do for Doug, he doesn't swim but he
does like to
see others do it as long as they've got tits,
legs all the way up and blonde hair, and who can
blame him?
These didn't have, and they glared,
I think they're called faggots,
I mean I know they're called faggots and I think
these were,
so we came here, Sunset Boulevard, and he's
drunk, well merry,
merry! He's never merry. He's looking at his
typewriter and so

I came out to look at our hotel from the outside
and be where
the Garden of Allah was,
very disappointing, they've put up a bank,
if it was here, but isn't it wonderful?
too hot of course and I've brought all the
wrong clothes and that
man is looking at me,
strangely,
because I'm talking to myself; "Hello... "
now he's looking away in disgust, Bogart type
but smaller, how small
was he? Did he seem small? I can't remember,
was he? But they do
such wonderful things with height in Hollywood,
don't they?
I hate lifts,
look up there! They're painting it out. I
wanted to see that film.

Thank God it's not one of Doug's!

Screech of tyres and shouts as she crosses Sunset Boulevard.

How easy it is to cross the road here,
everything just stops...

Elevator

Enter BARBARA. She goes up.

BARBARA: Don't you? Hate lifts?

We got stuck in a lift in an earthquake once
in Turkey
making the remake of "Scott of the Antarctic",
never got a release though it looked good,
sounded good thanks
to Vittorio and Sibelius, you won't have seen it,

nobody has, not General Public, at
any rate... I very nearly died,
only having Angela with me stopped me, she's my
daughter, same height,
darker, brown eyes, twenties, walks like a
dancer, we can wear the
same clothes, could, English Rose type totally,
but you won't meet her,
she isn't here, with us, you see we decided this
time to come on our
own. There wasn't an alarm and the old actor
we were with
fainted, after all day in the sun, and snow,
and nobody came when we shouted,
they don't do they,
that could be my motto,
some of them used to go blind from the glare of
the snow, in the
film, it came in trucks, salt actually, I think,
I love all that
don't you,
actually I'm sure they could hear us shouting
but as per usual nobody
had been paid, and they're all related in these
silly countries
aren't they? I say silly not in
respect of the country, I mean it in respect of
films, the silliness
of our being there, I shouted and shouted, we
did, I couldn't break
down in front of Angela...

Getting out of the lift.

I beg your pardon? No thank you...

*She says, nodding quite
pleasantly to someone who*

has said something to her
and entered the elevator as
she leaves.

Suite

Discovered DOUGLAS.

Enter BARBARA.

BARBARA: Doug, did you just see a tall man with a bald head, very brown,
in a lightweight rumpled suit?

DOUGLAS: No.

BARBARA: Forties? Don Ameche type? Was he tall?

DOUGLAS: No.

BARBARA: I did. He said, "Want a fuck?"

DOUGLAS: Did he?

BARBARA: Yes. Just like that, someone I've never seen before in
my life, white shoes, gold bracelet, no tie,
getting into the lift...

DOUGLAS: You hate lifts.

BARBARA: I know.

DOUGLAS: Did he bring a bottle of champagne?

BARBARA: I don't know.

DOUGLAS: Somebody did.

BARBARA: How nice. And flowers. From "Cynthia". How very nice of her.

DOUGLAS: What did you say?

BARBARA: No thank you.

DOUGLAS: Good, so he won't be back.

BARBARA: It was awfully nice of him to ask. Everybody
is so nice here.
Douglas! You've started writing.

DOUGLAS: The sooner I start, the sooner I finish.

BARBARA looking at DOUGLAS
behind his typewriter,
apparently naked.

BARBARA: You can't have started, you're drunk. You never
write when
you're drunk.

DOUGLAS: I do here. And I'm not. Three hotels later
he wasn't.

BARBARA: Are you going to put any clothes on?

DOUGLAS: I've got clothes on where it matters.

BARBARA: Who is Cynthia?

DOUGLAS: I haven't the faintest idea.

BARBARA: Are these flowers for you or for me?

DOUGLAS: What does it say?

BARBARA: "And for your bride". Have you got married?

DOUGLAS: Only to you, and that was ages ago.

BARBARA: What can Cynthia mean?

DOUGLAS: That's what they call wives here – brides.

BARBARA: How silly, dressed in orange blossom for ever...

DOUGLAS: Damn! I wanted to see that film, and they're
painting it out.

BARBARA: Shout! Perhaps they'll keep it on for you.

DOUGLAS: Hey! Too late. Television. It has become
   television with the stroke of a brush.
   What have you got there?

BARBARA: Postcards.

DOUGLAS: Good, get them off straight away.

BARBARA: But we're just off the plane...

DOUGLAS: I hate getting back before the postcards.

BARBARA: You promised not to start until you'd had a rest.

DOUGLAS: I've had one. Where have you been?

BARBARA: I went down to the pool, because I know you
   like to sit by
   the pool. All the English stay here. This hotel
   is famous for English.
   They didn't seem to be English... don't you
   think high heels
   look so odd when you're half naked?
   Doug, I feel so old. (*BELLHOP knocks and enters.*)
   Doug, I've got nothing to wear.

   Enter BELLHOP, small, old,
   Mexican type with seven
   large blue sensible and
   heavy Globetrotters on a
   trolley. He takes them
   into the bedroom.

DOUGLAS: We brought raincoats, wear a raincoat; and
   tweeds, and hats
   and sweaters and sensible shoes, I only just
   stopped you bringing your
   leg warmers didn't I?

BARBARA: You said you wanted to be very Wilfred Hyde
   White and Cary
   Grant English, tweeds, deerstalker...

DOUGLAS: I didn't, I said they liked that, English
    upper class tweedy.

BARBARA: You are not upper class tweedy.

DOUGLAS: No, but I've got the clothes, thank you. Thank
    God I packed
    my white trousers.

BARBARA: You can't wear those. You'll be laughed at.

DOUGLAS: Very Wilfred Hyde White.

BARBARA: Being laughed at?

DOUGLAS: No, cricket.

BARBARA: They're too tight for you.

DOUGLAS: Everything is.

    *BELLHOP stands and smiles
    at them. DOUGLAS glares at
    him.*

BARBARA: I've still got nothing to wear.

DOUGLAS: You can wear my white trousers.

BARBARA: I can't. They're so old fashioned, flared...

DOUGLAS: Thank you. Old fashioned, flared is good
    enough for me, the
    laughing stock of the studio...

BARBARA: Which studio?

DOUGLAS: Eh?

BARBARA: They wanted to know downstairs, at the desk.
    I thought it was
    marvellous, romantic, the manager asking which
    studio.
    except I expect they ask everyone, even ordinary

people, I expect
they make a thing of it, even though they know
most people aren't
with a studio, I expect people like it, expect
to bump into famous
faces in every corridor,
because of Bogart having slept here,
and all the others, think of anybody, here they
have slept,
and still do,
if they couldn't get into the garden of Allah,
across the road, or both, rooms in both,
from one to the other, not too much traffic then
that sort of thing; but I didn't know what to
say because there isn't
one is there, a studio? I mean it would be
silly of me to have said
Twickenham wouldn't it, the only one you go
to wouldn't it? So I said
nothing. I mean, who are you working for?

DOUGLAS: WBL, you know that.

BARBARA: Is that Al?

DOUGLAS: Yes, that's Al.

BARBARA: I like Al.

DOUGLAS: You've never met him.

BARBARA: He's nice on the phone. What does WBL stand
for?

DOUGLAS: Leg Before Wicket backwards.

BARBARA: No, really.

DOUGLAS: Really? I don't know really...
Wagner, Bean and Lentl.

BARBARA: Really?

BELLHOP: On the 1am I hear.

They both look at the BELLHOP
who is smiling wearily.

BARBARA: We must go out and buy you something. We
need a good guide book.
You ought to wear something for maids.

DOUGLAS: I will, for maids. But they won't look, you'll
find they know
how to keep their eyes where it isn't, look at
him...

BELLHOP: Just what I heard. You don't want to let it
worry you.

BARBARA: Shouldn't you give him something?

DOUGLAS: Yes.

BELLHOP: Why not?

BARBARA: Mostly because he's mean.

BELLHOP: Come on, he cannot be that mean.

BARBARA: Well, yes he can.

BELLHOP: I find that very hard to believe.

DOUGLAS: Have a nice day.

BELLHOP: Okay!

The BELLHOP shrugs, laughs and
exits.

BARBARA: Everybody is so nice, even when you aren't.

DOUGLAS: Should I have given him something?

BARBARA: He was so jolly...

DOUGLAS: Jolly?

BARBARA: Downstairs. I told him to wait until he was
    sure we were not
    going to come down again like we had at two
    other hotels and he laughed
    in a very jolly and carefree and understanding
    way.

DOUGLAS: Mexican. They are. Carefree and very jolly.
    I should have given him something because he
    has probably come illegally
    and been shot at and lives in awful squalor...

BARBARA: Uuuuuugh! Don't sit on this sofa in your
    white trousers.

DOUGLAS has got up from his type-
writer and is lurching towards the
door into the corridor after the
BELLHOP.

Exit DOUGLAS.

You haven't got any money!

He hasn't got any money. He's so mean he
won't carry money.

Re-enter DOUGLAS.

DOUGLAS: I haven't any money.

BARBARA: I know you haven't.

DOUGLAS: I should have given him something. It's just
    that I was so down.

Suddenly.

I can't be bothered with rushing around tipping
people. I've got work to do,
and so have you.

BARBARA: What have I to do?

DOUGLAS: Concentrate on me, on what I'm doing.

BARBARA: Vile Bodies is what you're doing,
   you are rewriting your adaptation of Vile Bodies
   which you were very pleased to be asked to do
   because you love the book and you said it wrote
   itself; because it didn't write itself the first
   time you rewrote it...

DOUGLAS: Good, yes, good, that's a start, though I knew
   that. I always take the precaution of writing
   the title page first, then you can't go wrong...
   Vile Bodies... go on?

BARBARA: What do you mean, go on?

DOUGLAS: Come on Barbara, I know what it is, what I'm
      writing,
   rewriting again... but what did I say I would do?

BARBARA: When?

DOUGLAS: When I said I would do it?

BARBARA: You said over your dead body.

DOUGLAS: Yes I know, but after that, what over my dead
      body,
   remind me, I've done other things since I died...

BARBARA: Over your dead body you agreed to change the
   leading character, Adam; who, in the book
   and in your first draft, and in your rewrites
   to your first draft is very English and a bit
   of a wimp into an American and therefore less
   of a wimp,
   so that, in inverted commas: "... we would have
   somebody to root for!"

DOUGLAS: Over my dead body.

BARBARA: Or the film won't be made.

DOUGLAS: Do I want it made? I earn a perfectly good
living writing films that aren't made, don't I?
In fact I probably earn a much better living than
writers who do have their films made... don't I?

BARBARA: I wouldn't know. I do know that unless you
have a film made soon people are going to ask:
"Douglas Who?"

DOUGLAS: They do.

BARBARA: I know they do, but not in the business, in
the business you are still reasonably well
known...

DOUGLAS: No I'm not.

BARBARA: Has it happened?

DOUGLAS: When?

BARBARA: Yes.

DOUGLAS: The other day, got it straight between the eyes
ears, on the
phone... "Douglas who?"!

BARBARA: Who?

DOUGLAS: Some frightfully well brought up tart in some
office all of sixteen.

BARBARA: Ah, too young.

DOUGLAS: I know. How do I earn a living Barbara?

BARBARA: It is quite amazing.

DOUGLAS: Isn't it?

BARBARA: And there must be others. Like you.

DOUGLAS: Quite. I know three.

BARBARA: It must be very frustrating for you...

DOUGLAS: It is... what?

BARBARA: Writing such good stuff and never seeing it made.

DOUGLAS: Eh?

BARBARA: Isn't it?

DOUGLAS: That's the sort of idiot thing said at parties... you're my wife.

Barbara, you don't have to say arsehole things like that, that's people
who know nothing about it... no it isn't
frustrating.

You know I'm not full of that every word a gem lark shit, you know that...
It is frustrating though...

BARBARA: There you are...

DOUGLAS: When they don't pay you as well as don't make it.

BARBARA: That's not frustrating, that's criminal.

DOUGLAS: It is.
The last time anybody said that to me it was
at one of those very boring parties we drove to
in London,
always a mistake,
she held my hand and looked into my eyes and
said how frustrating it must be for me...
it was, you were looking...

BARBARA: Oh yes... your fan.

DOUGLAS: What was her name?

BARBARA: I don't know, she was your fan.

DOUGLAS: She was a very famous and very beautiful British actress.

BARBARA: What was her very famous and beautiful British
name then?

DOUGLAS: Liv something... anyway she was right, used to be
right, not right anymore.
I find nothing frustrating, but I do get bloody
angry, I changed, it happened when I made fifty...

BARBARA: Fifty what?

DOUGLAS: Fifty years, you silly bitch.

BARBARA: Ah, that's supposed to be traumatic.

DOUGLAS: You wait.

BARBARA: You keep threatening me with wait. Douglas
I've been
fifty for six months longer than you have...
what am I waiting for?

DOUGLAS: It hasn't hit you yet.

BARBARA: It hit you the year before, repeatedly.

DOUGLAS: Yes, you're right, I slowed down, didn't I.
The thought made me slow down, didn't it. Then
I picked up again, didn't I? Found I could
do things with the other hand that's why...
things like gardening.

BARBARA: You don't garden, you pick up twigs.

DOUGLAS: Kindling, I gather kindling. Then I picked up
didn't I?
Three scripts in as many months... all exactly the
same I seem to remember, might have trouble there.
If just one of them gets made, I'll have to find
some way of destroying the others; and the producers
who employed me might get together. They do, you
know, they seem to have very little sense of self
preservation or pride, producers, have you

noticed? They congregate, they have guilds...
I know we do as well, but we rarely assemble
do we? They do.
Should my three producers assemble it would be
disastrous if they found out they had identical
scripts give or take a century, or give or take
a character, or worse start blurting out their
favourite lines... snap! I bought that!

No it wouldn't matter, they don't listen to
each other, not once they've got the credits,
they do early on when they're young and
picking up trifles, anybody's trifles... I
despise producers.

Don't you though?

BARBARA: No, I don't. I don't despise anybody.

DOUGLAS: Yes you do.

BARBARA: I despise you.

DOUGLAS: No you don't Barbara, you couldn't live with
me if you did, and I seem to
remember you are living with me, I seem to
remember that, the last time we were
anywhere in surroundings we had anything
to do with creating.

Remember you.

BARBARA: That was only yesterday.

DOUGLAS: And 8 hours, everything here is yesterday and
8 hours, or less 8 hours. Whatever it is,
it isn't real, that's why we're all lopsided
and that feet three inches above the ground
feeling...

BARBARA: I haven't got that.

DOUGLAS: Everybody else will have, this is where
  they sniff, puff, swallow,
  gobble, shove things into themselves just
  to have.

BARBARA: They were very interested in my hot flush
  tablets, weren't they?
  Did you notice? "Are these on prescription?"
  I'd hardly swill them down my throat every day
  were they not, they're the size
  of doughnuts, and I've
  got a very small throat.

DOUGLAS: Did you say that to the Customs man
  Barbara?

BARBARA: Yes I did.

DOUGLAS: Did he look at you strangely, Barbara?

BARBARA: Yes, but they all do. You'd be nothing
  without me and my small throat, things
  like that, as you have made a very good
  living out of showing...

DOUGLAS: I am bored with writing about you.

BARBARA: I could very easily become bored with you!

DOUGLAS: I didn't say I was bored with you, I said I
  was bored with writing
  about you. Everybody writes about you now,
  but who did you first? Me. And
  they're all doing you better than me, or
  rather they're all being more
  successful at doing you than me, making more
  money, more critical acclaim.
  I did you first. But am I given the credit
  For inventing you?

That first play of mine about you was seminal.

BARBARA: Who else is doing me?

DOUGLAS: They all are, to a greater or lesser extent.
Every play you see
has you in it.

BARBARA: I can't be in everything.

DOUGLAS: Everything.

BARBARA: I can't have been in "Ipi Tombi".

DOUGLAS: ... I didn't see that. You must have
been in Major Barbara.

BARBARA: Certainly in "The Dumb Waiter".

DOUGLAS: Liv Brown.

BARBARA: Is that what they do?

DOUGLAS: That's her name. That girl at the party, held
my hand and said how
frustrating it was for me...

BARBARA: She wasn't a girl. She was quite old actually
otherwise she wouldn't have known you.

DOUGLAS: I've always thought she was a marvellous
actress, haven't you?

BARBARA: Who is Cynthia?

DOUGLAS: What is she?

BARBARA: What we could do is have something to eat.

DOUGLAS: Which one of them is next?

BARBARA: Lunch.

DOUGLAS: I thought we had that last.

BARBARA: I don't know I didn't have anything.

DOUGLAS: I think I had too much. Did you bring
lots of bran?

BARBARA: I'm glad I wasn't asked about that. I think
Cynthia must be something
to do with the film.

DOUGLAS: Yes.

BARBARA: They're being very nice.

DOUGLAS: At this stage they usually are. They can turn.
Not so much turn... ignore.

BARBARA: After all they do want you to rewrite a
perfectly well written in the
first place film, they ought to be nice...

DOUGLAS: You work like mad for some two or three
weeks earning more money than
a real worker earns in as many years...
and you have three copies made, and
you send it in to Hawaii...

BARBARA: Hawaii?

DOUGLAS: That's where the last one went.

BARBARA: I'd forgotten that one...

DOUGLAS: ... and dull thud. I hope I addressed it
properly.

BARBARA: That was years ago.

DOUGLAS: Well it's a long way.

BARBARA: All those conference calls. I didn't know
what a conference call was
until you did that film, hello Los Angeles,
hello Honolulu, hello New York,
this is Banbury and then everything went
dead...

Every night.

At least you got paid, that's something.

DOUGLAS: So they must have got it.

BARBARA: I quite missed those conference calls when
they stopped.

DOUGLAS: They might have said.

BARBARA: Perhaps they're slow readers.

DOUGLAS: They are. Angela was only seventeen. And
this one, well they're being very
generous, first class out...

BARBARA: First time I've been first class...

DOUGLAS: Are we first-class back? Look at the tickets,
the buggers, they
would, I'm not going back if we're not first
class... yes I am, I'd bloody
swim.

BARBARA: I'm perfectly happy. Here we are in one of
the best hotels in
the world... well...

DOUGLAS: You've noticed the hissing?

BARBARA: Yes.

DOUGLAS: The radiator. Must complain about the pipes.

BARBARA: Very old... perhaps they do steam like that
in America, even though
it is very hot outside, the very hissing
heard by Helen Hayes, Leslie Howard,
William Holden, Howard (Hawks.) ... owww!

DOUGLAS: Isn't it?

BARBARA: Really Doug, you must try and enjoy it.
That was the whole point
wasn't it?

And it is quite funny, being here, you and
me sitting here in this crazy hotel

that calls itself a Chateau... must
complain about the pipes...

DOUGLAS: That's funny...

BARBARA: Yes, yes... sitting here, the sun beating
through the windows, those girls charging
down on us, leaping across that confection
of palm trees and signs and icing sugar
buildings shouting
... what are they shouting Doug?

DOUGLAS: "Yamaha".

BARBARA: No no, on the skyline, cut outs of girls,
they don't look like girls, they look like
stallions...

DOUGLAS: That's the California look.

BARBARA: Is it? I can't read it without my specs.

DOUGLAS: "Yamaha". It's an ad.

BARBARA: Oh. Well, that's funny, isn't it? And you
running after that Mexican bellhop in your
underpants, me with my suitcase full of
sensible tweeds...

DOUGLAS: Swimming trunks. Get it right. You are now
up the
sharp end and with me Barbara and you will
now see what it is all about. I won't have to
go through all that boring telling-it-at
dinner parties, because you are with me and you
can tell it yourself, the way it is, the way you
see it, the way you always do tell my stories
better than me once you've heard the original and
got word perfect,
even I laugh because I've usually forgotten them,
and anyway it's always the same story:

what is his story after all if it isn't the same
story? Hollywood, screwed by moronic producers,
money the
master, silly goings on in the movie industry...
well, while you're at it inventing the stories
invent this one, invent what I said I would do
once the airplane stopped speeding me through
a haze of first-class claret and I actually faced
page one, for God's sake Barbara, what am I
writing?

BARBARA: Are you all right?

DOUGLAS: No, I am not all right. I know where I am,
I just don't know what next to say, or rather I
know what next to say because it is here before
me, but... what's wrong with it, Barbara? It
seems all right to me. Why am I here to write
it again?

BARBARA: Money?

DOUGLAS: Yes.

BARBARA: They probably won't pay you anyway.

DOUGLAS: There is that. No, they always pay... something.

BARBARA: People get very bored with highly paid screenwriters
complaining.

DOUGLAS: What a thing to say!

BARBARA: Don't they though.

DOUGLAS: I expect so.

BARBARA: You're not all right.

DOUGLAS: I am never all right. I'm a simple chap. I
used not to bother, just do the work, and
take the money, but just lately I've
begun to have doubts.

BARBARA: Why don't you wait for them to come over
and talk?

DOUGLAS: Oh no, it's the talking kills it.

BARBARA: Where are you going to talk?

DOUGLAS: I don't know. In here?

BARBARA: Where do you want me to go?

DOUGLAS: When?

BARBARA: When you talk to them.

DOUGLAS: Next door. I want you next door, listening
to every word, I want you to listen
to everything I say and then I'll know what
I'm talking about... you can
tell me later when they've gone.

You won't need that.

*Throwing her book across the
room.*

You haven't come here to read books.

BARBARA: How do you manage when I'm not with
you?

DOUGLAS: When you're not with me by now I'd have
finished it. I usually get straight
on with it. Twenty pages at least before
they come and I can open the door to
them with a smile on my face...

*The telephone rings. They are
both struck dumb and rigid.*

*After a moment DOUGLAS says
through clenched teeth.*

Get it!

BARBARA: Me?

DOUGLAS: You.

BARBARA: Why me?

DOUGLAS: Get it...

BARBARA: Got it.

She has picked it up, listened,
holds it for him to hear.

There's nobody there. I got it –
nobody there...

DOUGLAS: You didn't get it fast enough.

BARBARA: You don't care.

DOUGLAS: I do care.

BARBARA: Why did I have to get it anyway?

DOUGLAS: I might not be in.

BARBARA: Where would you be? They've just paid
thousands of pounds transporting you
here, where would you be?

DOUGLAS: Anywhere. I could be anywhere. I have
a life of my own you know.

BARBARA: Do you want me to keep got it, or
put it down?

DOUGLAS: You always get it at home.

BARBARA: I'm on holiday.

DOUGLAS: Thank you. I bring you all this way to
look after my interests and as soon as
you arrive you announce you're on
holiday.

BARBARA: Aren't I?

DOUGLAS: To some extent, yes...

BARBARA: You said, and don't deny it because Angela
　　was there, you said: "Come with me it'll
　　be a holiday for you."

DOUGLAS: My very words. Doom laden.

BARBARA: Guilt laden. No, that's unfair, not in your
　　case. I thought when you said it, guilt,
　　but I knew it not to be the case, you'd
　　have said it better because you'd have
　　thought about it...

DOUGLAS: Isn't it?

　　Going to be... ?

BARBARA: When I can get hold of a good guide book and
　　go and see things.

DOUGLAS: Don't leave it lying around, if you do,
　　take it with you, but... who is going
　　to answer the phone if you're intent on
　　sight-seeing?

BARBARA: You are.

DOUGLAS: Not if I'm working. The phone is over
　　there, and I'm over here getting
　　what I can of the sun, by the time I
　　reach the phone it will have stopped
　　ringing.

BARBARA: Well, good...

DOUGLAS: The phone only rings thrice in Hollywood,
　　think of the future, girl,
　　one, two, three,
　　and if Douglas Who isn't got then it's
　　get me Joe Whatsisname, Jerry Thingumajig.
　　Even now that call not got by you is

being got by somebody who should have been
me, a big easy film... even now they're
laughing, discussing availability,
money even, and I've missed it...

BARBARA: But you've got a film, you're rewriting it...

DOUGLAS: This is the time to get the next one, when
you've got one, they're not interested
in you if you haven't got one...

DOUGLAS strides.

BARBARA: You're foaming at the mouth!

What's the matter with you Douglas?
What have you become?

DOUGLAS: Hollywood Man. It takes a little time.
But, what you see before you is he. This
is the way you have to be here. One two
three hi!

BARBARA: One two three what?

DOUGLAS: Hi.

*He throws himself on the sofa,
reaches for the phone.*

One two three and "Hi!"

*He picks up the phone, says
into it:*

Hi. Yes – I'm sure he'd be glad to talk
to you about it, why don't you let him
call you when he's not so busy writing
the one he's got now... have a nice day.

*Putting the phone back just
as a voice from the hotel desk
says: "Hello, can I help you?"*

*Then picking it up again and
saying.*

And I think Liv Brown would be ideal for
the part.

BARBARA: That's not her name.

And even if it was somebody, you never pick
up the phone until it's rung
long enough for you to know they're not
going to give up, and you go
ashen, and you can't be interested in the
future, your future is two
more rewrites and a polish...

DOUGLAS: A polish! There you are, you've caught it.
Hollywood Woman,
talking of polishes...

BARBARA: Don't you turn on me. I'm your only friend
here, I'm your only
friend anywhere Douglas Thingummy...

DOUGLAS: Nonsense! I've got friends. I'm always
supposed not to have any
friends, by you. In fact I'm the one who
has got friends, and as it happens
most of them are in Hollywood.

BARBARA: Actors!
You can't call them friends. Just you try
and stop one on the street... Douglas
Who?

DOUGLAS: Not just actors, directors and other people,
real people. The last
time I was here I made a very good friend
of a cab driver who liked roses.

BARBARA: There isn't a telly. There must be. There
isn't.

*DOUGLAS lying on the sofa in a
very awkward position, his
attention caught by something
out of the window and above
BARBARA's head.*

DOUGLAS: He asked me did we have roses in England.
They ask the oddest things
when they get friendly. I meant to send
him a catalogue. I'm sure he didn't
believe me.

BARBARA: I wanted to see some television in America,
at least.

DOUGLAS: You won't have time for television...
one, two, three "Hi!"

BARBARA: I see. I shall say hello...

DOUGLAS: Well, you risk losing the movie, baby, but
say hello if you want to,
we can sub-title it afterwards...

BARBARA: Why are you lying on the sofa in that
impossible position?

DOUGLAS: My spine.

BARBARA: What about your spine?

DOUGLAS: This is the only position affords me relief.
Open Cynthia's champagne.

BARBARA: I can't bear warm champagne.

DOUGLAS: Then put it in the fridge and order some
cold champagne, no... better
still ask them if they'll do a swap...

BARBARA: God, you're so mean.

DOUGLAS: I know. That poor little Mexican bellhop.

BARBARA: Quite.

DOUGLAS: It's terrible. And they're dying in trucks
    here you know, desperate to
    get to the land of the free, crammed in
    layer on layer, false bottoms,
    which is why I will never travel anywhere
    other than first class.
    But he vanished
    Barbara, honestly... he was gone so fast.

BARBARA: I'm not surprised, are you? Chased by a
    near naked fifty year old
    who can't stop clutching his privates...
    anyone would vanish.

DOUGLAS: You never do.

BARBARA: I don't have to. I'm your wife. You
    really are lying there in the
    most extraordinary position.

DOUGLAS: I'm stuck.

BARBARA: Which bit of you has gone?

DOUGLAS: All of me. I'm transfixed.

BARBARA: I think Cynthia is probably a friend
    of someone.

DOUGLAS: No friend of mine. You know, I suspect
    that Cynthia may be trying to poach me.

BARBARA: I beg your pardon?

DOUGLAS: I've heard they're all women at the
    moment. They're all women in Hollywood
    at the moment running everything. I
    suspect she's after me...

BARBARA: What for?

DOUGLAS: I could be wrong but I think so.

BARBARA: Yes, but what for?

DOUGLAS: I suspect she's after me to look after me. I think I'll go and put some clothes on.

BARBARA: Why?

DOUGLAS: Because I'm not comfortable in myself.

BARBARA: I look after you.

DOUGLAS: I know you do.

BARBARA: You were very hot a minute ago.

DOUGLAS: Yes.

Exit DOUGLAS.

BARBARA suspicious. She puts herself into the position DOUGLAS was in on the sofa, not without difficulty, and sees what he was able to see on the balcony of the penthouse above.

BARBARA: Douglas! You were looking at that woman!

DOUGLAS: Of course I was.

BARBARA: I knew you were looking at something.

DOUGLAS: Isn't it amazing?

BARBARA: I hope you're getting dressed because you're embarrassed.

DOUGLAS: I am, I am...

BARBARA: You can come out now, she's sat down.

Re-enter DOUGLAS putting his clothes on.

Do you think it might be Cynthia?

DOUGLAS: That would be nice.

BARBARA: She's standing up again and stretching.
You've really got to suffer to see.

No wonder you felt embarrassed in your
Y-fronts.

DOUGLAS: Mmmm. Worth it though, not a stitch
on.

BARBARA: How painful it must have been for you,
Douglas, because it is excruciating,
isn't it? If I hadn't noticed, how long
would it have taken you to mention there
is a completely naked and very beautiful
woman standing on the skyline, and can
everybody see her?

Oh my God, close the curtains.

DOUGLAS: What?

BARBARA: Close the curtains, Douglas, do
something... I've never been so
embarrassed in all my life...
it's Robert De Niro.

DOUGLAS: Oh yes, so it is.

BARBARA: He looked straight at me.

DOUGLAS: Well, you can see why he's a star
can't you?

Poolside

*Poolside. Sound of voices. People swimming.
Not seen but heard. Two pools of
sun. One where the other people
are, another small one where
BARBARA is to come.*

Enter BARBARA dragging loungers.

BARBARA: His head for heights, I thought.
So, I came down here wearing as much as I
decently could, to the pool like a
maiden aunt, reading a book but really
listening... they are all English
as far as I can tell, but where they all
come from I really can't work out.

There's one that Douglas will like I think,
high heels, but not our sort
at all, very posh.

Enter DOUGLAS.

Ah, there you are.

DOUGLAS shedding clothes.

DOUGLAS: Yes, thirty pages later, there he was...

BARBARA: You are marvellous.

DOUGLAS: I am.

BARBARA: I've had to move twice to avoid that pile
of rubbish, I don't know
whether it's following me or not...

DOUGLAS: Thirty pages.

BARBARA: Good.

DOUGLAS: Soon be rid.

BARBARA: Don't say that. The last of the sun.

DOUGLAS: Who is that?

BARBARA: That's better, I thought you'd notice her.

DOUGLAS: Showgirl.

BARBARA: Something like that, looking for Errol
Flynn, not his writer.

DOUGLAS: It's the high heels, the white high heels,
    interested in children
    and will go back to being a doctor, nurse,
    beauty consultant when her reign is
    over, wants to be an actress, get into
    movies, work with people, meeting
    people, contradiction after contradiction...
    thirty pages...

BARBARA: Smokes like a chimney, that's why I had to
    keep moving, look, another
    little pile building up...

DOUGLAS: Thirty more pages tonight, and tomorrow and
    tomorrow night,
    soon be home...

BARBARA: Relax Douglas, I'm able to relax and do
    nothing for the first time in ages.

DOUGLAS: You're tight as a spring, soon be rid,
    soon be home.

BARBARA: I'm enjoying it. This must be what the
    Garden of Allah was like, apart
    from the people, lolling by the pool, the
    bungalows, there should be
    a model, in the book she said there was a
    model of it – I couldn't find one. But what
    would a model show, just the pool shaped
    like the Black Sea, and the bungalows
    what else? Couldn't show the names
    could it...?

DOUGLAS: The phone rang.

BARBARA: Yes?

DOUGLAS: Just once, didn't get it.

BARBARA: I can't stay in just because.

DOUGLAS: Quite, you're on holiday waiting for Charles
Laughton to rise out of
the Black Sea in his dripping hump, carry
you off, dripping, up among the
gargoyles... that is the oddest sight
isn't it?

BARBARA: Do you mean wide floppy hat with rather
wan child?

DOUGLAS: Yes I do.

BARBARA: They're all English.

DOUGLAS: How do you know that? They're all naked...

BARBARA: Isn't it amazing how you can tell? All that
cod liver oil after
the war. Is it good for tits? Didn't help me.

The one in the floppy hat is American I
think, with a rather strident
voice... listen...

*They do, for a moment in which
there is complete silence.*

She isn't doing it now but she was, loudly,
a minute ago, we all know her
business, impossible not to, she has been
called to the poolside phone
twice, and discussed incredible amounts
of money...

DOUGLAS: Is she suckling that child?

BARBARA: I thought that.
She hasn't up to now. She might.

DOUGLAS: Well I think it's quite worrying that
nobody has tried to phone us.

BARBARA: They have, I was there.

> She has been trying to persuade pop star
> with gold earring, at least from
> his conversation he is but who and how
> pop only Angela in our immediate circle
> would know and she thank God is beginning
> not to care... that she can do
> wonders for him, Floppy Hat, he's tired,
> Gold Earring,
> all night I suppose,
> anyway Floppy Hat can do wonders for him,
> he is being handled very badly at the
> moment it appears, still... the amazing
> thing is while she was telling the wonders
> she was going to do for him she
> was fully dressed,
> when he agreed she could she stood up and
> unzipped and flopped full frontal apart
> from floppy hat and I thought wonders to
> perform but she didn't,
> and is now totally ignoring him,
> hasn't done a thing for him since she took
> her clothes off,
> they have hardly looked at each other,
> oh they're still friends but distant,
> hardly say anything at all... the
> other thing is there is a black man who is
> fascinated by it all...
> he keeps peering through the bushes,
> up there... I'd hate to call him a Peeping
> Tom... look... too late,
> he's gone.
> Funny woman, Floppy Hat, she's still
> got it on.

DOUGLAS: You know, I think we are mad to want to stay
here when there are much

cleaner ones,
with flowers on a tray and fruit,
that's your Garden of Allah,
and they bring room service on a white table-
clothed table, the whole
covered with a vast sheet of cellophane...

BARBARA: No, this is it. Oh that poor dog!

One of them has a poor dog, terribly thin, it
roots in the rubbish and eats fag
ends, it's so sad.

DOUGLAS: Where?

BARBARA: Gone.

DOUGLAS: Don't keep getting me to look up Barbara,
I'm trying to get some sun.

BARBARA: It belongs to one of the girls in one of the
bungalows. Where Nicholas Ray edited his
last picture...

DOUGLAS: Where?

BARBARA: One of them, in one of them.

DOUGLAS: I wish I'd seen it.

BARBARA: I didn't.

DOUGLAS: Has it been on television?

BARBARA: I don't know. Are you going to sleep?

DOUGLAS: Trying to...

BARBARA: That dog is shitting in the bushes.

DOUGLAS: Must be getting enough to eat then.

BARBARA: It's skin and bone.

DOUGLAS: I've got an awful feeling you're going to do
something about it.

BARBARA: I think I ought to.

DOUGLAS: No, please.

BARBARA: One of those groupies has it. They don't
come out until the day is
nearly gone like slugs, nothing on under
cotton, dreamy eyes... faint whiff of joss...

DOUGLAS: Slugs come out in the rain.

BARBARA: These would, they'd stand in it...

DOUGLAS: They sound quite interesting.

BARBARA: You wouldn't like them, dirty knicks...

DOUGLAS: Not if they haven't any on, Barbara.

BARBARA: When they have them on. Aren't you cold?

DOUGLAS: Who is that English actor?

BARBARA: Where?

DOUGLAS: The one sitting by the board.

BARBARA: Really, Doug you must know him, he was in one
of yours...

DOUGLAS: I know, – I just can't remember his name...

BARBARA: I refuse to tell you, you must try to
remember names, Doug it's all
names...

DOUGLAS: I remember Liv Brown.
I just can't remember his. It was years ago.

BARBARA: You didn't like him anyway.

DOUGLAS: John? He vanished didn't he?

BARBARA: Came here I expect. Doing awfully well now
I expect.

DOUGLAS: He must have seen me, why is he ignoring me?

BARBARA: More interested in her.

DOUGLAS: That's grand.

BARBARA: She's a reporter.

DOUGLAS: How do you know Barbara... she seems a
perfectly ordinary naked woman
to me...

BARBARA: There he is?

DOUGLAS: Who?

BARBARA: That black man. Look. Oh, too late,
he's gone...

DOUGLAS: Have you thought he might be looking at you?

BARBARA: Me? I'm respectable.

DOUGLAS: Perhaps that's it. Perhaps he can only
get off on every inch covered.

BARBARA: Are you trying to get me to take my clothes
off for protection?

DOUGLAS: No Barbara. Even though at your age you
might have a point.

BARBARA: You look awful.
You can't get into those swimming trunks.

DOUGLAS: Then how did I?

BARBARA: You may have got into them but it wasn't
wise. You must be in agony.

DOUGLAS: Only if you keep making me twist about.

BARBARA: Do they do this everywhere in Los Angeles?

DOUGLAS: What?

BARBARA: Take their clothes off at the drop of a hat?

DOUGLAS: Barbara, don't shout.

BARBARA: I'm not. Don't fuss.

DOUGLAS: I'm not fussing, you are making a very
loud fuss.

BARBARA: They're all too bound up with themselves to
notice, they all think they're
frightfully important, don't they, with
their rock bands and their films and
their Oscars... you've written more films
than they've seen let alone been in...

DOUGLAS: Films has nothing to do with it. They're
probably all accountants,
that sort of thing...

BARBARA: Really, with their clothes off? Is that what
they do – go into their offices, add up
a few columns and then take their clothes
off?

DOUGLAS: If there's any sun, yes, and if they've
finished their work, yes...

And why not?

BARBARA: Go on then, sit up and have a good look...
go on, you know you
want to.

DOUGLAS: Don't be silly.

BARBARA: Go on.

DOUGLAS: I would rather not.

BARBARA: How anybody can think that it's attractive...

DOUGLAS: The last time we were in America together
we saw a Topless Mother of Eight,
do you remember?

BARBARA: We did not. We saw the sign for her. In neon.
Why on earth anyone would
want to see a topless mother of any number...
why would that be a draw?
What do you think she did? Play skiffle on
her stretch marks?

It was that long ago.

DOUGLAS: Well now they're topless by the pool, and
bottomless, it's been
happening for years Barbara...

BARBARA: And on balconies and on the skyline...

DOUGLAS: You're obsessed with nudity!

It means nothing any more, nothing at all, it
is totally uninteresting...

BARBARA: You're interested.

DOUGLAS: Of course I am interested, I'm a fifty
year old man.

BARBARA: That black man is interested again, through
the bushes... if it's
so uninteresting, why is he so interested?

Bedales.

DOUGLAS: Pardon?

BARBARA: Those girls, they're on holiday from Bedales
or somewhere, wearing their regulation green
cossies... I suppose he plays with
himself.

It must be half term.

DOUGLAS: Half term and out to L.A.?

BARBARA: Why not? These people are rich Douglas...

DOUGLAS: We're here – we're not rich... if I were
   rich I wouldn't be here.

BARBARA: Or they're being paid for, as we are...

DOUGLAS: Who?

BARBARA: The Bedales girls in their regulation cossies.

DOUGLAS: I didn't know Bedales had regulation anything,
   isn't that the attraction? Didn't somebody we
   know think of Bedales and then decide not to
   for what he was going on in the long grass,
   or with the long grass...?

BARBARA: Look. I think it's so funny the way everyone
   steps over the flat one, you did. She
   doesn't look well to me, did she look well
   to you?

   Look...

DOUGLAS: Barbara, I do desperately want to see
   everything you're telling me but I don't
   want to see Bedales girls in their...

BARBARA: That's why you will never write anything
   decent for films, you can never see the
   ironies...

DOUGLAS: Yes I can.

BARBARA: No you can't, otherwise you would see the
   irony of a completely naked and bored
   housewife of a money juggler from Richmond
   sitting on the edge of a pool in
   Hollywood without a thought in her head,
   her two children by an undoubtedly previous
   splashing about in the pool wearing their
   regulation cossies...

   Their friend dying at their side. Flat.

DOUGLAS: Why do you assume not a thought in her head?
Do your thoughts drop to the floor with
your clothes when you take a bath?

BARBARA: Not even reading a book.

DOUGLAS: Other peoples thoughts not even in her head.

BARBARA: They don't belong to you writers exclusively,
just because you've had the luck to find them,
they become our thoughts no matter how hard
you try...

DOUGLAS: That's why I write films. I refuse to be
responsible.

You can pin nothing on me.

BARBARA: The irony is that the little Bedallions
realise they are the odd ones out and keep
pulling their straps down, their mother keeps
pulling them up again. There he is again.

DOUGLAS: Don't give me irony. Irony's not bankable.

You know I think the one in the floppy hat
could be Cynthia, if she's an agent.

BARBARA: Look at them all like maggots in the corner
where the last drop of sun is.

DOUGLAS: Well it isn't here.

BARBARA: Go and snuggle up with the maggots then.

Look at them.

Why don't I go upstairs and ring you?

DOUGLAS: Why?

BARBARA: Just look at them... they've all had phone
calls, all except the flat one, all of them,
why shouldn't you have a phone call?...

most of all Floppy Hat has had phone calls,
she's flopping up and down to the phone all
the time one two three hi...

It makes me so pissed off. They ought to be
ringing you!

DOUGLAS: Barbara, don't shout – who ought to be
ringing me?

BARBARA: Everybody ought to be, the world, the work
you've done, the world, reporters, producers,
WBL.

DOUGLAS: WBL should.

BARBARA: What's the matter with WBL? Thirty pages,
you are good Douglas, thirty pages and they
don't even care. I must say you are good when
you decide to be, you really do stick
at it... but don't work all night? Let's go
out and have a funny foreign meal somewhere.

That very white flat one hasn't moved all
the time I've been out here, have you seen her
move?

I haven't. I expect she's been to the
Maharishi, on another plane... flat.
Look at that stomach, legs flat as
sat-on cigarettes, flat as a slab...

DOUGLAS: Yes, do go and ring me.

BARBARA: That's all right. I was beginning to
worry, she jerked, did you see her jerk?

DOUGLAS: No, don't.

BARBARA: Oh God, she's having a fit!

Not much of a one... her friend has
noticed, so that's all right.

The poolside phone rings.
DOUGLAS cowers.

DOUGLAS: That's for me.

Second ring. He shudders.

Someone just walked over my grave.

BARBARA: Would be nice if it was for you.

DOUGLAS: No it wouldn't, why would it?

BARBARA: Floppy Hat has got it.
So she can't be Cynthia.
It is for you, she's waving it at you.

DOUGLAS: Ignore her. I am not ready to talk to
anyone.

BARBARA: I am ignoring her. She is still waving
it.

DOUGLAS: How does she know it's for me. How does
she know I'm me?

BARBARA: You don't think they don't know. They all
know. Vaguely. The vampires.

DOUGLAS: I can't.

BARBARA: Go and get it. You must.

DOUGLAS: No, it's no good... I can't.

BARBARA: Why can't you?

DOUGLAS: I've just looked. It's the telephone.

BARBARA: What do you mean?

DOUGLAS: I find the sight of a telephone in the
hand of a totally naked woman unaccountably
arousing. I've got an erection, therefore
I can't stand up, do you mind?

BARBARA: Not at all. Would you like me to get it?

DOUGLAS: If you would be so kind.

BARBARA: The erection or the phone.

DOUGLAS: Both.

BARBARA: In what order?

DOUGLAS: Whatever is most convenient.

BARBARA: Shame, never mind, perhaps we can
recreate the moment. So...
one two three...

Hello? We say hello... ah Cynthia...
yes, I'm the bride, along for the ride...

No – Can I take a message?

She laughs, then gasps,
shaken by what she sees
looking across the pool.

Oh my God. Mouth to mouth, mouth to
mouth on flat legs!

I don't want to die in Hollywood,
Douglas, do you. It would be awful
to wouldn't it?

Sound of an ambulance
siren heard.

The curtain falls.

ACT TWO

Sunset Boulevard

The following day.

The curtain rises.

Enter DOUGLAS.

DOUGLAS: Yes I do.

*He says to someone, nodding
quite pleasantly.*

Just one very good one before I die
but I don't think it will happen with you,
thanks all the same. You know they're so
cheap, the hoardings,
not the girls,
I was saying one day how much I had always
wanted to have my name up on
a hoarding on Sunset and the producer I was
with said he had too,
until he found out how cheap it was,
then he didn't want to have his name up
there any more,
but it would have to be so small anyway,
it isn't our names people want to see,
it's names like Robert Redford, Paul Newman,
Rita Hayworth,
say some more Douglas,
names like Dustin Hoffman,
more, well names like Martin Sheen, Robert de
Niro, he already gave,
Meryl, er... what's her name...
ah – Streep, Meryl Streep,
but anyway they're so cheap, and if you
really wanted it you could have it.

I'm very worried about WBL, they haven't
said anything at all,
except Al, any of them, not Wagner, not
Bean, not Lentl,
except Al before we came out,
he wants Jerzy to direct it,
he loves Jerzy like a son,
soon as he said that, I knew Jerzy wouldn't
get it, Al has got a son, he never sees his
son, because he hates his son,
I love Jerzy like my son,
Jerzy you blew it... but with Al anyway
you have to get to him early,
before some other guy?
no, before lunch, because like after lunch
he just doesn't make sense,
but he never seems to be drunk, sir,
names like Richard Gere,
... where are we in all this, Barbara
and me?

He puts his hands up in the
air, continues:

Do you know in all the time I've been coming
to America this is the
first time I've been mugged,
just about to be if they don't find enough
money in my wallet,
there's nothing you can do about it, just give
them the money,
give them everything, the lot, let them look
through it and take what they want.

They are both so ordinary looking, in very
expensive looking silver bomber jackets,
a T shirt with Honky Tonk Freeway on it;
there isn't anything you can do, one of them
has a knife but I don't think

he'll use it,
the other has a gun and it's pointing at me
now, but I don't think
he'll use it.
I think it could go off... I'm sorry there
isn't very much in the wallet,
we're being paid for by WBL we hope...
some English money but that's no
use to you is it? Oh! You can use it? Oh,
that's nice... really? Well
it depends on when you're going but at the
moment King Lear, Much Ado, and Derek
Whatsisname in the Tempest.
Well, if you can use it, you're welcome,
have a nice day.

Thank you, sir. Do I just walk away?

Exit DOUGLAS

I don't think I'll tell Barbara

Suite

Discovered Barbara unpacking clothes.
Enter DOUGLAS.

BARBARA: How was that?

DOUGLAS: Odd.

BARBARA: Why?

DOUGLAS: Funny lady.

BARBARA: Cynthia?

DOUGLAS: Yes.

BARBARA: Did she make you laugh?

DOUGLAS: No.

BARBARA: Did she make you drunk?

DOUGLAS: No, I did that myself.

BARBARA: Let me see... ? Don't lie.

DOUGLAS: I felt like it.

BARBARA: You said funny.

DOUGLAS: I expect so.

BARBARA: Later you mean when we tell it?

DOUGLAS: I expect so. Odd, certainly. What did you do?

BARBARA: Unpacking.

DOUGLAS: Totally unsuitable clothes.

BARBARA: It does rain. And it does get cold. People
     slide down mountains here
     in the rain, the lot, house and pool and
     grand piano...

DOUGLAS: Grand piano?

BARBARA: If they have one.

DOUGLAS: What else?

BARBARA: Nothing much, read my book, tried to find the
     television. There must be one.

DOUGLAS: Anybody phone?

BARBARA: No.

DOUGLAS: No! NO!

DOUGLAS erupts in anger.

How much work have I done? Look at it, pages
of it... eh? And not so much as
a hello... a hi... not one bloody phone
call...

BARBARA: Perhaps you ought to phone them...

DOUGLAS: It isn't up to me to phone them. If I phone
them where would we be?
I've gone at least fifty pages beyond phoning
them... it would be disastrous
now to phone them... we could still be here
next week Barbara. I want to get
on and get it done, get out of here...

BARBARA: They've sent flowers.

DOUGLAS: Where?

BARBARA: There.

A huge flower creation,
still in its cellophane wrapping.

And fruit.

DOUGLAS: Where?

BARBARA: There.

An equally huge fruit creation
still covered with cellophane.

DOUGLAS: I don't want flowers, I don't want fruit...
I want to go home.

BARBARA: And there's a car in the garage for you.

DOUGLAS: I don't want a bloody car. I don't want to go
anywhere. That's what they want us to do,
waste time... Barbara I've seen a man in a
mink-lined jacket – in this weather.
Nobody phoned at all?

BARBARA: No.

DOUGLAS: We come half way round the world, I work like
a black...

BARBARA: We've only been here since yesterday.

DOUGLAS: Long enough.
Are you sure nobody has phoned Barbara? It
would be just like you not to answer...

BARBARA: Nobody has phoned Douglas.

DOUGLAS: I don't understand it. They want their pound
of flesh don't they, eh?
They want me to relax, listen to them...
they want me to talk and talk and
bloody talk...

BARBARA: Not yet they don't, otherwise they would
have phoned.

DOUGLAS: They don't work here you know. They get up
do a workout at the gym,
have breakfast, wander across town, talk to a
screenwriter or two, set him
back at least twenty pages, stroll out to
lunch, play squash, swim, lie by
the pool, give him a ring and put him back
another six, go to a party, see
a screening, laugh about it, have dinner,
ring him up and ruin tomorrow's
output... that's what they call work...
they won't get down to it. Good solid
page after page...

BARBARA: They don't seem to be doing any of that.

DOUGLAS: No. It's very odd. Those flowers are very
ugly.

BARBARA: Aren't they? I think they're something very
nasty and tropical like
we have at home under the yew tree, I thought
I'd leave the wrapping on until
we were sure...

DOUGLAS: Sure of what?

BARBARA: Well you know what they smell like at home...

DOUGLAS: They won't smell of anything, and the fruit
won't taste of anything,
you'll find... go on... try...

BARBARA: You look shattered.

DOUGLAS: I am.

BARBARA: Was she awful?

DOUGLAS: No.

BARBARA: What was she?

DOUGLAS: Small, slim, tough, dark, Judy Garland type...

BARBARA: That's how you like them. Young?

DOUGLAS: Painted.

BARBARA: All over?

DOUGLAS: She didn't take her clothes off.

BARBARA: Won't she have to?

DOUGLAS: I expect so, Barbara.

BARBARA: To be in the swim?

DOUGLAS: Very good Barbara, I expect so.

BARBARA: You didn't sign anything?

DOUGLAS: No.

BARBARA: Ah, there you are then...

DOUGLAS: There I am then, what?

BARBARA: One two three flop... as soon as you sign,
you should have signed.

DOUGLAS: Yes.

He goes to the window, hot,
tugging at his tie.

I am not dressed correctly.

BARBARA: For what?

DOUGLAS: Anything, here...

BARBARA: So *you* took your clothes off...

DOUGLAS: No, Barbara.

BARBARA: Why is your tie crooked then?

DOUGLAS: My neck.

BARBARA: They all do it here, don't worry... take
their clothes off.

DOUGLAS: You're still going on about people taking
their clothes off.

BARBARA: I know I'm obsessed with it.

DOUGLAS: I said you were. Why?

BARBARA: Because I've got a scrawny old white fifty year
old body, that's
why, and nobody else in this whole fucking country
has, nobody...

That's why.

Thirty years. And when I was beautiful and young
and could show you, thirty years
ago I was shy and you've never seen it properly
and now this whole country is
naked, all beautiful...

DOUGLAS: It does seem that way.

BARBARA: And I hate it and I wish I had never come.

DOUGLAS: Never mind.

There's nothing you can do about it. It doesn't
seem so bad in Banbury does it?

BARBARA: Now when I've got the nerve to do it it's too late
because it's
awful.

DOUGLAS: Mine is too.

BARBARA: That isn't the same thing.

DOUGLAS: Never mind.

She had this thing in the corner. Cynthia. The
phone never stopped ringing.

BARBARA: One two three... ?

DOUGLAS: Faster than that, the greed!

BARBARA: What did you have for lunch?

DOUGLAS: You know how you always laugh at me, both of
you, when I say
"scallions"?

BARBARA: Yes we do. It's the way you say it. As if it
had "rap" in
front of it. Where?

DOUGLAS: I don't know where. There was a drunk Irishman
kissing everybody and
giving them champagne... he looked very ill,
white, wet black hair, nicotine
lip, Dylan Thomas type... it's the place to go,
they all go there and have
scallions. I did. No, I tell a lie. We went
out of there because Cynthia was
insulted and went somewhere where we had scallions,
somebody thought she
was a whore she said, hooker she said, which

is the same thing,
fascinating derivation but I don't believe it,
I hadn't noticed, but she had.
You know what I'm like I never notice anything
when I'm terrified.

We had, I had tabbouleh, which is...

BARBARA: I know what tabbouleh is, I cook.

DOUGLAS: ... Middle Eastern and is tomatoes, parsley
and scallions. The
scallions are coming back. They grow their own,
the first to do so in the
whole of Hollywood so I'm told, I said I'd been
doing it for years but
she didn't believe me, she expressed great interest
and I knew she didn't believe
a word I said.

They don't believe you when you tell the truth
about ordinary things, growing
vegetables, liking home, but they do believe you
when you say the most extraordinary
things about films, writing them, the amount of
work you're doing, the number of
pages you've written, how much you care about
what they think...

BARBARA: Yes, you are shattered aren't you?...
so am I, I think. Come and sit down.

DOUGLAS: Look. He's back.

BARBARA: Who is?

*DOUGLAS at the balcony window
looking down, opening the doors,
joined by BARBARA.*

DOUGLAS: Your black friend of yesterday, behind the
hedge.

BARBARA: I know. He keeps walking round. I've watched
   him. I think he's employed by the hotel...

DOUGLAS: What to do? Look?

BARBARA: My God, he's looking straight up at me.

DOUGLAS: He is. Straight through me.

BARBARA: I feel naked.

DOUGLAS: Success, now we can go home. He's done it, he
   can now claim a raise,
   and get it.

BARBARA: If I move he'll think I've noticed him.

DOUGLAS: Exactly.

   You're stuck. At his mercy, little black
   face looking up.

   There he is behind a hedge, and there,
   over there is the whole of the strip,
   crawling with it, just crawling,
   they even advertise. Hey, Barbara, look
   what I found.

BARBARA: What is that?

DOUGLAS: I thought it was the comic strip section
   of the Los Angeles Times. It isn't. Not
   exactly. Listen to this:

   (1.) Come come come for any position in
   private rooms open Sunday.

   (2.) Exclusively Nude in Orange County.
   Kiss me all over outcall.

   (3.) Present this ad between the hours of
   6 a.m. and 2 p.m. and receive bonus
   gift.

(4.) I'll sit on it if you'll call me over.

(5.) For a piece of Class and stimulating conversation from England with Love.

(6.)Most cards. Major cards. All cards.

(7.) Join the Hot Love Rite of Real Church...

"Hallelujah!"

and he peers timidly over a dusty hedge at English ladies and gents and their agents, little black face.

And *that* is why people go to the movies. Isn't it? It's all the same thing. The looking is all!

BARBARA: I'm going to wave at him.

DOUGLAS: Why?

BARBARA: Then he'll go away.

DOUGLAS: You can't be sure.

BARBARA: Oh my God, he's waving back.

Do something Douglas.

DOUGLAS waves as well.

BARBARA: You shouldn't have done that.

DOUGLAS: Did the trick, he's gone. He didn't want to be waved at by me.

BARBARA: But he'll be back.

DOUGLAS: But you won't be there.

BARBARA: You waving at him has made it all right, he'll come back and look straight up here.

DOUGLAS: Expecting to be waved at?

BARBARA: Yes, yes... you shouldn't have let me wave
at him, you shouldn't
have.

DOUGLAS: I didn't let you wave.

BARBARA: You waved.

DOUGLAS: That's what you've got to do, take no
notice of them...

BARBARA: Taking no notice isn't waving.

DOUGLAS: Wave, it's showing them it doesn't
matter.

BARBARA: But it does matter.

DOUGLAS: Why does it matter?

BARBARA: That's how these things happen. You know
how these things happen, Douglas.

DOUGLAS: This is a true story.

You'll like Cynthia, she's an animal lover,
she had one in the corner, rough
carpet a foot thick, plate glass, chrome,
and chunks of stone with precious
glittering scoops taken from them, and
this thing in the corner, huge, sitting up,
paws together neatly, the size of a small
horse, this dog...

Dead.

She said "Hi Douglas, say hello to
Stanley" and I regret to say that
I did.

I sat in the corner with Stanley and I
patted him on the head and said "Hello
Stanley".

He likes me. She said she could tell
he liked me by the space around us.

The space around me and a dead dog in
a corner, stuffed. It was loved
so it got stuffed, not very well...

That's life.

I suppose I was seduced.

BARBARA: You didn't sign anything? I knew I
shouldn't have let you go. Douglas
you already have an agent...

DOUGLAS: She's awful, but she can get me more
money than I've ever had before,
she said she could come to some agreement
with my present agent
she said they are very good friends,
she said they do everything together
when he's here,
she said they go to the beach, Santa
Barbara, Barbara,
and I was thrown, yes really thrown by
the fact that she so obviously
seemed to want me, and when they want
you... I don't know...
what else is there?

BARBARA: Why does she want you?

DOUGLAS: I don't know.

BARBARA: Has she read anything?

DOUGLAS: Yes, everything.

BARBARA: There's a catch in it.

DOUGLAS: I don't know, funny woman, and Stanley, after
Stan Laurel, I could see that.

BARBARA: How could you?

DOUGLAS does his STAN LAUREL
face.

There's a big catch somewhere. What about your
own agent?

DOUGLAS: She is my agent.

BARBARA: Douglas she isn't. Douglas you didn't;

DOUGLAS: Here. He can be my agent there, in Banbury.

He should be here. He is never where I want
him.
He ought to be here ringing them and asking
them why they're not ringing
me, not me, it isn't up to me to ring...

She knew all about it. She said she'd heard it
was brilliant. I asked her
how she knew that when I had not as yet finished
rewriting it brilliantly
and she said that that was the word.

She had got the word that it was brilliant.

That's what I call an agent. He could have
told me that...

BARBARA: You can't say he hasn't got you enough money,
first class flight, me
included, expenses and a fee and flowers and
fruit and a car... I wasn't going
to tell you about the car.

DOUGLAS: Why weren't you?

BARBARA: They're very down on drunk driving here.

DOUGLAS: So they are everywhere, I'm not going to drive
when I'm drunk.

BARBARA: It isn't drink with you, it's to do with how
high you are, and I don't
want to be driven by you, not here...

DOUGLAS: Well it's impossible here without a car, it
really is.

BARBARA: Well if you've got one, in the garage downstairs
and if I were you I'd leave
it there...

DOUGLAS: Have you read it?

BARBARA: Yes. It's fine but page one is missing...

DOUGLAS: It'll be somewhere.

BARBARA: Good, yes I thought so, and anyway not the end
of the world.

DOUGLAS: Have you had the windows open?
That's it... it's blown out of the window,
every time you open the door when the
windows are open... whoosh! The whole
lot... whoosh!

BARBARA: You're striding. Sit down and keep still,
you're striding.

DOUGLAS: I know I'm striding.

BARBARA: Don't, because later on you'll feel awful, you
know you will.

DOUGLAS: Don't keep on about me being high. I'm not
high.

BARBARA: You are.

DOUGLAS: Well, if I am it's for a very good reason...

BARBARA: Yes, Cynthia.

DOUGLAS: No, not Cynthia. Not just Cynthia, not really,
I wish you'd been there, Barbara, they're so

rich here, all of them, really rich, and she
says that one film could keep me for a year
here...

BARBARA: You will be very ill. You know that don't you.

DOUGLAS: I expect so.

BARBARA: Why don't you do your Alexander?

DOUGLAS: Thousands of dollars – it was all Thousands and
Thousands of dollars. Straight for my Achilles
Heel, straight for my weakest point. She held
my bollocks in her hand, Barbara, she really did,
and she's awful, but... no, it's no good,
I can't do it without Angela to feel if I'm
relaxed.

BARBARA: I'll do it.

DOUGLAS: Angela is my daughter, you are not. You tense
me, she doesn't,
listen to me, I'm all tense and you haven't
touched me,
Alexander will have to wait until I get home...
She's one of those people who make overtures,
Barbara.

Cynthia.

It's hopeless, I'm like a coiled spring...
money you see, money... I react
to money like others react to...

*DOUGLAS on the floor with his
knees up, head flat on the
carpet.*

BARBARA kneeling down with him.

I don't know, I don't know what other people
react to, I only react to money and

sex, yes I do react to sex... don't touch me
look at me tense...

It's no good.

I need a book under my head.

BARBARA gets one.

Not a paperback, a real book, a thick one, did
I bring my dictionary?

BARBARA: Only the Readers Digest Pocket.

DOUGLAS: Won't do, not high enough. Get something else,
phone book, I can
see right up your skirt.

That's it. You've got to get brown.

I want you brown all over and in the proper
clothes... we'll go and buy some
clothes.

BARBARA: I don't want any clothes.

DOUGLAS: I want you in the proper clothes and brown all
over under it, them

I can't relax, you've teased me, standing over
me... that would tense anyone.

BARBARA: Don't be so rude.

DOUGLAS: Come on, I'm not staying here where I'm not
wanted, let's go somewhere.

I'll get the car out and we'll go somewhere...

BARBARA: Where is there to go, Douglas?

DOUGLAS: There's everywhere to go. Don't you want to
see your Garden of Allah?

BARBARA: It's gone, there's nowhere to go.

DOUGLAS: We can go anywhere, the beach, everybody goes
    to the beach, to San Diego, we can eat...
    again... have you eaten?

BARBARA: Yes.

DOUGLAS: Where?

BARBARA: I asked them in the hotel, Oscars, just across
    the road, everybody goes there, so I went...
    You can get steak and kidney pie.

DOUGLAS: I haven't come all this way for steak and
    kidney pie.

BARBARA: I had Lancashire hot pot.

DOUGLAS: Why?

BARBARA: Because I'm terrified, Douglas!
    For no reason. The place is as familiar as
    Saturday afternoon and old films. The language
    the same. Am I frightened in London? I
    probably am. We did see somebody die by the
    pool... there is an existence here which
    doesn't seem to include us, I'm frightened
    of that... aren't you?

DOUGLAS: Yes, I understand. I know.
    When Cynthia had finished with me I was
    wet with sweat...

BARBARA: Your clothes...

DOUGLAS: I know, but... before when I've been here
    I haven't felt it. I suppose it's having
    you here.

BARBARA: I knew I shouldn't have come.

DOUGLAS: No no... I wouldn't have come without you.

BARBARA: Why didn't we just say no. What you're doing
    here you could be doing at home.

DOUGLAS: You've never been to Hollywood.

BARBARA: I know.

DOUGLAS: You are enjoying it really though, aren't you?

BARBARA: I'll be all right.

DOUGLAS: You see, unless you're with me I'm useless, I
wouldn't be able to do anything
if you weren't here, look at what I've done
already... how many pages?

So you see I'm sort of terrified too. But
we've come all this way and we've got to
be brave.

BARBARA: Why?

DOUGLAS: Because it's going to get worse I think.

BARBARA: I'm so ungrateful. I really am.
People envy us
being here...

I hate it.

DOUGLAS: I can see.

BARBARA: I'm sorry.

DOUGLAS: You must try.

BARBARA: Why?

DOUGLAS: Now we're older we must be braver, wilder, try
harder... it isn't
enough to have the credits.

BARBARA: Are you sure?

DOUGLAS: Yes, I feel that we shouldn't.

BARBARA: You are a good driver.

DOUGLAS: I don't think you ought to say that.

BARBARA: I had my fingers crossed.
Well, you're not bad anymore, you used to be,
now it will have to be very bad luck, or mind
on other things.

DOUGLAS: No, sometimes completely.

BARBARA: They come so fast.

DOUGLAS: We'll start by going round the block getting
used to the right hand
side of the road.

BARBARA: Oh God...

DOUGLAS: Just the same as driving in Frence.

BARBARA: I know.

DOUGLAS: So.

BARBARA: But you won't drive in France.

DOUGLAS: That's because of Frenchmen.

BARBARA: You won't drive to Banbury on Saturday nights
and that's because of
American men in their Air Force.

DOUGLAS: Quite. But here I speak the language, so do
you, should it come to
explanations... that's the problem with the
French, the explanations.

BARBARA: You ought to be working.

DOUGLAS: Do they really think that! Have they thought of
ringing up and saying I
ought to be working? I worked all night... do
they know, do they care?

Where do you want to go?

BARBARA: Hollywood Boulevard.

> I found a little map. Look... it isn't far
> we could walk.

DOUGLAS: Why do you want to go to Hollywood Boulevard.

BARBARA: Graumans Chinese Theatre, Myrna Loy. I've
always loved Myrna Loy... I
want to see her feet.

> Yes. You ought to have some fresh air. We'll
> walk, it isn't far.

DOUGLAS: No, we'll drive. I'm sure it's longer than it
looks on the map.

BARBARA: If it is we'll come back.

DOUGLAS: We'll drive...

Exit DOUGLAS determined.

BARBARA: Douglas... I don't think we should.

Exit BARBARA after him.

Garage

Sound of car being revved.
Enter BARBARA.

She stands and waits.

BARBARA: Have you seen the gutters? They're so dirty.
One doesn't expect
California to be so dirty but the gutters are full
of rubbish. Huge drains. I
suppose it all flushes away in one big suck and
glug every now and again...

She steps back from a grating.
There is a shout and the
sound of a car horn.

Douglas is not finding it easy to get out.
He has hit two concrete pillars.

Crash.

Three.

Slam of car door.
Enter DOUGLAS.

DOUGLAS: We'll bloody walk!

Exit DOUGLAS.

Exit BARBARA.

Street

Enter DOUGLAS and BARBARA
walking towards Hollywood
Boulevard. The noises of
Sunset Boulevard are still
heard but as if through a
filter.

BARBARA: Isn't it strange?

DOUGLAS: What?

BARBARA: Walking.

DOUGLAS: Yes.

BARBARA begins to whisper.

BARBARA: All the houses look empty don't they?

DOUGLAS: They're not.

BARBARA: No. Little old ladies hiding in them. I don't
like the shutters on
every window and door, do you Douglas?

DOUGLAS: No, I think we've made a mistake.

BARBARA: There's a huge hoover on that lawn. They hoover
the lawn.

DOUGLAS: It's not grass.

BARBARA: What a good idea.

DOUGLAS: Let's go back.

BARBARA: Why?

DOUGLAS: Look up there... look down there... you do
realise that we are the
only people in the street, in the whole street.

BARBARA: Where is everyone?

DOUGLAS: I don't know.

BARBARA: Does anybody live here?

DOUGLAS: I imagine so.

BARBARA: I think we ought to turn round and go back.

DOUGLAS: Right. Which way?

BARBARA: I don't know which way, let's ask.

DOUGLAS: Who are you going to ask?

BARBARA: I'll knock on the door and ask.

DOUGLAS: Barbara, come back... Barbara...

He goes after her.

... it isn't a good idea. Look up the street.
A police car.

She waves at a cab.

DOUGLAS: Don't. It won't stop.

BARBARA: It hasn't, why not? It didn't have a fare.

DOUGLAS: They don't.

BARBARA: Why not?

DOUGLAS: I don't know, they just don't.

BARBARA: How silly.

DOUGLAS: Yes. Let's just keep walking, away.

BARBARA: I'm going to ask the policeman.

DOUGLAS: No, Barbara, don't.

*He grabs her arm and pulls her
back.*

BARBARA: Yes I am, why not?

DOUGLAS: Because it isn't a good idea.
This is the way, come on...

BARBARA: You're wrong, I remember that hoover, this is
the way.

DOUGLAS: Please Barbara, this way...

BARBARA: You have no sense of direction.

DOUGLAS: Yes I have.

BARBARA: This is the way...

DOUGLAS: This way...

*With his eyes still on the police
car he grabs hold of her and runs.*

Screams from BARBARA.

BARBARA: Douglas, you're hurting.

DOUGLAS: Stop struggling then...

Exit BARBARA and DOUGLAS.

Whop-whop-whop of police sirens.

Suite

*The whop-whop-whop continues on
the Strip below. Night. Shouts
and laughter from the Strip.*

BARBARA: Oh...

DOUGLAS: We were arrested, Barbara.

BARBARA: I know, I know, they were so rude, Douglas.

DOUGLAS: They thought we were criminals Barbara, or
rather they thought I was
a criminal and you were a madwoman.

BARBARA: They were so nice until I mentioned WBL and Al.
Then straight up against the wall and tearing my
clothes off like demented beasts...

DOUGLAS: It was bound to happen.

BARBARA: ... searched, just because I mentioned Al.

DOUGLAS: Yes.

BARBARA: Did you?

DOUGLAS: Yes, I did.

BARBARA: I didn't know his second name. They refused to
believe I didn't
know his second name. But he always calls
himself just Al.

DOUGLAS: Yes.

BARBARA: Did you know his second name?

DOUGLAS: Yes I did.

BARBARA: But you never remember names.

DOUGLAS: I know. But when I needed it my lack of memory
proved to be no
friend, remember that, crystal clear it came out;
Al J Franco Jr, and there
I was up against the wall, me, my legs, feet being
kicked so far apart my spine
shrieked... and they'd already done me once at
the car, you can vouch for that
Barbara.

BARBARA: Why?

DOUGLAS: Oh, didn't they tell you?

I am a dupe, Barbara. I think I am a screenwriter,
not really a good screenwriter any more, just an
average one who earns a reasonable living writing
films which are never made, like we all do, that's
all... but I'm
not, I'm a dupe...
I tried to explain my curious way of life
but they didn't understand.
You'd think they would... here... of all
places...

BARBARA: I know. You would.

I did my best. What does he do. What does he
write? What does he make?
They do know what screenwriters look like
here, Douglas.
They know, and we don't look like screenwriters
Douglas, unsuitably dressed going about our
business persons like us Douglas.
They looked at me odd when I told them how long
we had been married, too long Douglas,

and only once Douglas,
and screenwriters are winners here Douglas,
they ride,
one film and from then on they ride. I told
him we would have ridden could you have driven
and no, not drunk, perplexed, introspective,
bewildered, out of mind, abstracted,
he put down drunk all the same,
and looked at me, not the right shape, the
right age, the right style, or the right
story,
me, thrown up against a wall and searched,
me, wrong clothes, wrong me,
handbag, purse, handbag, purse.
Come on for Christ sake, this guy is a
screenwriter?
and kindly would I explain my life with you,
what kind of money do you make?
and I told them, large sums,
usually dollars, were talked of often...
that you sat at a desk and wrote and
rewrote deserts and wastes
and once you wrote seventy thousand horsemen
coming over a ridge and laughed for
weeks,
and once you wrote enter Hitler and could
never get over the thought that perhaps
you should not have done,
but I told you if you hadn't somebody else
would,
and you were probably a spy,
nothing for you to get a phone call one day
and be in some exotic silly sounding place
the next,
clutching gibberish,
rewritten gibberish,
for Arabs among others, never seen again,

just the sound of seventy thousand laughing
horsemen,
the jungles of Borneo you'd been to
the streets of Santa Fe,
never for longer than it takes to get out
of the aeroplane,
hand over the worthless documents, be told
they won't do
get back aboard again,
they never do,
but large sums certainly change hands,
or banks,
and people with foreign accents are
frequently bloody rude on the phone,
and I cry and you storm but still you
do the rewrites of the rewrites and
that it's a trade,
they don't have to be made, for a long
time you can live on one, just one that
has been made.

And that wasn't it fun?

And then he asked me the cruncher, Douglas,
the one they always do,
what had you written he might have seen?

And he was very young, Douglas,
he can't have seen anything, nothing has
been made for years, ten years,
we don't mind because life goes on and
you're still asked to do the rewrites
of the rewrites but it does seem very
odd to ordinary people...

Criminal even. Like you said.

DOUGLAS: What?

BARBARA: Earlier...

DOUGLAS: Did I?

I'm a dupe it seems, not a screenwriter at all,
nothing more than that,
a fool... a front.

For Al, and Wagner, and Bean and Lentl.

I suppose some sort of fraud. Definitely fraud,
but they wouldn't tell me what,
they hoped I might tell them, then they could tell
me and prove my guilt, that
sort of thing, definitely fraud, is it any wonder
nobody phoned, they were
fleeing the country, on the run, is it any wonder
they did not have time to
phone... I have to go down to the police station
tomorrow with what I have
been writing, before they decide whether or not I
am a dupe, a fool, or... an
extremely clever man. I'm not an extremely
clever man, Barbara.

The only problem is, I've never had to submit a
script to the police before,
I don't know the market. What will they expect
to read?

Cynthia was a great help. She said she could vaguely
remember me as an English
writer of the sixties... I was there when she
phoned. I heard her.

We should never have gone for a walk. That is
what started it all. People do not
walk about the streets in Los Angeles.

BARBARA: They do. That lot out there, listen to them
screaming and laughing,
and all last night... I couldn't get to sleep
for them.

DOUGLAS: They're criminals.

BARBARA: I know.

DOUGLAS: Don't tell anybody, ever, whatever you do... the
shame!

BARBARA: No, no I won't.
Lock the door Douglas.

DOUGLAS: You lock it.

BARBARA: I want to make sure it is locked, properly.

DOUGLAS: It is.

BARBARA: Are you sure?

DOUGLAS: Yes...

   A knock.

BARBARA: Who is that?

DOUGLAS: I don't know, ask them...

BARBARA: Who is that?

   The door opens.

   Enter BELLHOP with a sheaf of
   papers.

BELLHOP: You know I don't want to worry you sir but you
really shouldn't leave your door open in this
crazy city...

BARBARA: No, I know...

BELLHOP: Do you have trouble with your spine sir?

DOUGLAS: Yes I do.

BELLHOP: I guess you do. You work too hard. You don't
mind me telling you
you work too hard?

You a writer? I know you're a writer. You work
too hard, relax, you want me
to help you relax?

I'm an expert at martial arts, I frequently need
to relax, just relax, let
your whole body go flat, here let me just get
you to relax here...

*The BELLHOP on the floor, working
on DOUGLAS's shoulders.*

Did you get busted?

DOUGLAS: Yes.

BELLHOP: WBL?

DOUGLAS: Yes.

BARBARA: Yes.

BELLHOP: I heard they was on the lam, they had it coming.

DOUGLAS: Did they?

BELLHOP: Sure thing, drugs, too many phoney movies
located in Columbia, girls,
... drugs, WBL?

BARBARA: We have nothing to do with all that.

BELLHOP: That's right. They owe a lot of money. You got
your plane tickets?

DOUGLAS: Yes.

BARBARA: Our film isn't set in Columbia. It's set in
London.

BELLHOP: Now see I'm just going to pull my hands away
and you must let your
whole body go flat see... how's that...?

DOUGLAS: Fine.

BARBARA: Are they going to go on all night again... down
    there, in the
    street?

BELLHOP: The hookers?

Yes ma'am, it's Saturday night.

Did you get to see Stanley?

DOUGLAS: Stanley?

BELLHOP: Sure, you got to see Cynthia? Stanley. You know
    when I first came
    out to LA I dated Cynthia a few times, you know
    she's crazy, you know she
    takes Stanley everywhere, and you want to know
    something? Stanley has
    always been dead. I don't know anybody who ever
    saw Stanley alive... weird.

You got an orgy scene in your movie?

DOUGLAS: No... er no I don't think so...

BELLHOP: "Vile Bodies"? Am I right? You got to have an
    orgy scene in a movie
    called "Vile Bodies", if you don't have an orgy
    scene people are going to be
    very disappointed.
    There is no way you're going to convince me
    that you are serious if you
    don't get an orgy scene.

BARBARA: The film isn't going to be made anyway.

BELLHOP: Oh come on, with this guy's credits?

On your front, Douglas.

*BELLHOP sitting astride DOUGLAS
looks at BARBARA with something
like scorn.*

DOUGLAS quite perks up. BELLHOP
gets to work on him again.

Come on, relax... it's not the end of the world,
right? So Wagner, Bean and Lentl
because of circumstances beyond their control
like criminal charges do get to
pass on it, so... some other guy one day in some
studio will say Christ what
have we got here, cease from contemplating he
should schtupp some person and
exclaim this script is good! Come on; look on
the bright side, you may get
lucky, come on, relax... you are still so
tense Douglas...

Did you make it with Cynthia?

DOUGLAS: I don't think so.

BELLHOP: Sure... you can try again when the heat's off
WBL, come on, this
year WBL next year MGM always some guy
skimming, somewhere, some kind
of phoney deal, they bounce back... keep your
eye on the ball, write a
good script... get an orgy... see, why I ask
did you ever write an
orgy? See, why I ask is, I do orgies.
You say, so what? This guy does orgies, he
should be so lucky.

But you can't just orgy. You say why the hell not?
Okay we got this orgy scene,
let's go? You get some kids want to be in motion
pictures, you give them two
three hours to work up something and then you
shoot... right?

It will be so dull.

You think you just need to hire some hookers?
It is so dull. They can do it,
they can have a really good time, and you can
shoot it, you can give them everything
they need, some kids in from the street and
whooooow! Right?

It is so dull. You see the rushes and you say
when am I going to get my
orgy you guys? Really rock bottom.

See you got to hire the best. I am the best.

You hire me, you get the best, we are pro's, we
just fly in, come out of
make-up, strap on and get to it,
no junk, no shit, no booze, and when you say cut
we roll off and we think
beautiful thoughts and when you say action we act,
and you think, this is gross, there is no beauty
here, there is no poetry,
this is totally gross, and you think when am I
going to get my orgy
you guys, when am I ever going to get my truly
beautiful orgy?! And you despair, you think to
yourself when will I learn that beautiful things
cannot be contrived,
orgies only happen when two or more people have
some special feeling
for each other or something... something like
end of shooting or
that super party at the office or something, you
don't just hire people
at great expense to come out from LA and simulate,
you are so depressed,
and we take our money and we leave with dignity...
and later on you steel
yourself to view the rushes and whooooooow!
They are terrific!

Believe me, they are terrific, fantastic, and I
swear to you that we do
nothing, nothing at all ma'am, nothing. It is
such a let down.

Until you get to view the rushes, and then you
say I got my orgy, whooooow!

Am I right?

DOUGLAS: Right.

BELLHOP: You bet.

BARBARA: There is one thing, I would like to watch
television...

BELLHOP: Pardon me?

BARBARA: There doesn't seem to be a television set.

*The BELLHOP goes to a bureau of
antique beauty and ornate Spanish-
ness and taking hold of one of the
false drawers BARBARA has pulled
at several times without success,
slides them open to reveal a huge
screen.*

Thank you.

BELLHOP: You're welcome.

*BELLHOP picks up his sheaf of
papers and finds a single sheet,
asks:*

Name of Adam? Right?

DOUGLAS: I beg your pardon?

BELLHOP: And the girl is called Nina, right?

*BELLHOP reads from the sheet of
paper.*

Adam: Who was it said that really divine things
      didn't happen?

Nina: I think I might have done. I don't think
      this is at all divine, it's given me a
      pain.

DOUGLAS: That's mine.

BELLHOP: Okay.

The BELLHOP sorts through the
other sheets of paper.

That's all I've got for you this time, there's
a guy in 403 uses
the same typewriter but he is not in the same
league Mr. Davies,
not in the same league...

Think orgy.

Exit BELLHOP.

BARBARA: He knew who you were.

DOUGLAS: Yes he did. He had scores of sheets of paper
    Barbara. I thought I
    heard another typewriter today.

BARBARA: Douglas. Let's go home.

DOUGLAS: I hope we can.

DOUGLAS at the table with his
script, finding the place to
put the recovered page in.

I'm still missing page one.

Do you know what? I bet this hotel is full of
us, pages fluttering
from the building all day...

BARBARA: Can you put something in front of the door?

DOUGLAS: Look at them down there...
All of them so young...

Shouts from down on the Strip.
Laughter of the girls, "Hi
Honey". Constant sound of the
cars on the Saturday night crawl.

How do you convince a policeman about something
like "Vile Bodies"? He
won't understand a word of it.

BARBARA: Douglas, lock the door and put something in
front of it, please.

She is shivering.

DOUGLAS: I'll have to finish it. They won't understand
it unless they've read the book, they won't
see what I'm getting at.

BARBARA: Look at the door Douglas, look all round it,
do you see where the doorframe has been broken?
Do you remember that
awful hotel in Germany where you pointed out to
me how you could see where
the door had been broken down.

Look.

DOUGLAS: I'll put the chair in front of it.

He does.

BARBARA: And the other one from the bedroom. The
other door. There's a fire escape
going down from that one...

DOUGLAS: This is ridiculous –
The maid will think we're mad.

BARBARA: And we're not, they are.

DOUGLAS: I don't think so, it's us Barbara.

*BARBARA looking down onto the
howling Strip. DOUGLAS coming
to join her.*

BARBARA: I'm going to ring Angela.

DOUGLAS: Yes, do... oh look at them down there,
hundreds of them
all so young,
look at them and the cars...

BARBARA: How do I?

DOUGLAS: What?

BARBARA: Ring Angela.

DOUGLAS: You know our phone number, surely.

BARBARA: Yes, but...

DOUGLAS: You can dial direct.

BARBARA: She isn't at home, she's staying with Jenny,
you know that...

DOUGLAS: Yes... all right, calm down...

BARBARA: Stop looking at those girls.

DOUGLAS: Ring Jenny, you know her number by heart...

BARBARA: Don't be so bloody rude, and stop looking down
there. What do I dial
first Douglas?

DOUGLAS: Four four...
And then the number... four four and then the
number with local code in
front of it...

BARBARA: All right, I'm doing it.

BARBARA dialling.

DOUGLAS: There's a helicopter over there.

BARBARA: Nothing happens.

DOUGLAS: Keep trying.

*BARBARA does. Again and again
while DOUGLAS stands at the
window.*

*Finally she picks up the directory
and looks for the number to call
the operator.*

Look they move in waves, the girls,
they struggle to get to the cars, hundreds of
them, I've never seen this before, I've been
here lots of times, not here,
in Beverly Hills, it would have been better for
you if we'd stayed in
Beverly Hills,
there, there is your Garden of Allah,
it's back, it's never gone, what if they
move towards us,
in waves, them and their pimps, and the
thugs in the cars? You've terrified me now.
Wave after wave of them... there's a searchlight,
they're lighting them,
they've got the set, they've got the lights,
the helicopter is lighting them from the air,
shouting,
orchestrating them, moving the waves of girls...

BARBARA: Hello operator, I want a number in England... yes,
that's London.
Moreton in Marsh four-oh-one...

No, it isn't in London. It's in Gloucestershire...
No, that's not in London either.

...M.O.R.E.T.O.N... in M.A.R.S.H

Four-oh-one.

DOUGLAS: It's amazing. Now they're all gone, every girl
has gone. Empty. Not a
soul to be seen.

Whop-whop-whop of police cars.

That's amazing. How do they do that?

BARBARA: Of course it exists, people live there. My
daughter is living there
with one of my very dear friends...

It does exist, it does exist!

I see.

I am not shouting at you! It does EXIST!

*BARBARA slams the phone
down. Calms herself and
says to DOUGLAS who is still
staring out of the window.*

BARBARA: There's no such place as Moreton-in-Marsh.

DOUGLAS: It's what I've always suspected.

BARBARA: Then where is our daughter, Douglas?

DOUGLAS: Now they've all come back, look, the pavement
is packed with them.

BARBARA: What do I do now?

DOUGLAS: Well I can't stay here looking at whores all
night... look at them.

BARBARA: What do I do?

*DOUGLAS goes to his typewriter,
looks at his script,*

puts a piece of paper into
the machine.

DOUGLAS: I've never written for a police department
before. Do I take all the swear
words out, or put more in?

BARBARA looks through the
directory. Reads:.

BARBARA: Survival guide? Have you seen in here? Survival
guide. In the front of
the phone book.

Child Abuse Hotline. Doesn't that make you
shudder. Zenith 21234
Dog Bites, Santa Monica 829-2911.

How to Handle Obscene Phone Calls. Don't answer
questions you wouldn't
answer if asked by a stranger in the street. I
did Douglas, that was
the first thing I did,
tall, forties, Don Ameche type, I answered him,
I said "No thank you" to a
question I wouldn't answer on the telephone in
the street, no thank you.

Earthquake! A whole page.

There will always be earthquakes in California.
Always... do not go sightseeing
afterwards...

Here it is, rape. I knew it would be. Rape
Hotline.

Where does it say how I get to ring my daughter?
Not anywhere... I wouldn't
want to ring her from here, look at them all
down there in the street,

none of them older than Angela,
and you were looking at them, weren't
you Douglas?

DOUGLAS: I suppose so.

BARBARA: Would you want to talk to your daughter from
here?

DOUGLAS: No.

BARBARA: This is the most dangerous place I've been in.
Do you know they were
teaching little old ladies how to kill, in the
police station,
I saw it while I waited to be stripped,
and searched,
just because of you, and WBL and where is he?
Al? Somewhere in the South of
France, on a yacht...

DOUGLAS: Well it won't be Cannes.

BARBARA: You think it's funny for little old ladies to
be going in fear of
rape?

He did, their instructor, let me welcome you
girls... all carefully called
girls though hat pin crumblies to a man,
welcome to the program,
let me tell you that when you graduate you will
be able to kill,
wow!
wow! from the girls, jokes and joshing from the
instructor,
and they loved him,
and they giggled and they flirted, and he gave
them a for instance,
how tall do you think he is Miss Plumptopp?

wow you got yourself a tall one there,
where is he, by the pool? How heavy is he
Miss Plumptopp? Wow, you
got yourself a heavy one there,
do you think you can handle it? Sure you can,
sure... colour?

You are quite right Miss Plumptopp, I stand
corrected, all muggers, rapists, sexually
deprived compensatory activated
persons are the same to us regardless of race
or creed, blow him
away grandma, or... mace him.

Three squirts ought to do it, but never forget,
leave one squirt in the can
for yourselves girls, and here's where we
consider your loved ones,
mace does not discriminate, so do not squirt
until you are sure,
and do not ever become blase,
there is great power in mace which must not be
abused,
there is a condition known as mace happy, I have
warned you about it,
I have told you of little Miss Wouldn'tthurtafly...
until she ran
amok that is, and there it was; two delivery
boys from Greenblatts on the
path, her masseur stretched across the front
door, her dachshund parboiled
in the hot tub... her husband in the garage,
he never made it out of his
car!... so, think before you squirt,
the yellow eyes which stare
at you, the terrible hands which clutch at
your body, the hot breath at your
throat could emanate from your husband...

Flash of light from outside.
From the helicopter.

What's that?

DOUGLAS: It's the helicopter.

DOUGLAS working hard, typing
furiously.

BARBARA: What's it doing?

DOUGLAS: Circling the hotel.

BARBARA: What for?

DOUGLAS: I don't know.

Perhaps there's somebody outside, climbing up
outside...

BARBARA: Do you think there is?

DOUGLAS: I don't know.

DOUGLAS stops typing. The
helicopter hovers very close
and they are both transfixed
by the light through the
windows.

Door knock.

BARBARA: There's somebody at the door.

DOUGLAS: I know.

BARBARA: Don't let them in.

DOUGLAS: Keep quiet then.

The door knock again.

We're all right as long as they can see us,
the police in the helicopter.

BARBARA: But we're criminals, Douglas.

DOUGLAS: Not really, we're working for the Police
Department now, the L.A.P.D., it'll all sort
itself out and Al will reign again,
they'll all sort it out...

*DOUGLAS smiles bravely in
the white glare of the searchlight, waves.*

Worse things have happened.

*As BARBARA waves the helicopter
swoops away fast.*

BARBARA: It's gone.

Door knock – door pushed open.

DOUGLAS: Quiet.

BARBARA: Somebody is opening the door.

*The door is opened and the
chair pushed aside.*

*Enter BELLHOP with a wrench.
He makes straight for BARBARA,
tugs her to the open window,
shoves her head out, waving
the wrench.*

BELLHOP: Stand there!

BARBARA terrified.

BARBARA: Yes... yes... please...

*Bellhop waving his wrench
at DOUGLAS who stands
halfway towards them.*

DOUGLAS: Don't...

BELLHOP: Sniff!

BARBARA: What?

BELLHOP: What can you smell?

BARBARA: Smell?

BELLHOP: Sniff.

They sniff.

Freshly baked bread, right?

BARBARA: Yes.

BELLHOP: This is the only place you can smell it, some
trick of the air. Is
it not wonderful, fresh baked bread like momma
used to bake... huh?

BARBARA: Thank you.

BELLHOP: You're welcome.

BARBARA: You're so... nice...

BELLHOP: Don't mention it. Ma'am I want you to know,
I never penetrate, I'm
a pro.

*BELLHOP feels in his pocket
brings out a sheet of paper,
very crumpled, smoothes it,
hands it to DOUGLAS.*

Exit BELLHOP.

BARBARA: What is it?

DOUGLAS: My first page...

BARBARA: Douglas, shouldn't you give him something?

DOUGLAS: I suppose so...

BARBARA running after the
BELLHOP.

BARBARA: My husband wants to give you something...

DOUGLAS: No no Barbara, don't go out there...

BARBARA stops.

BARBARA: No.

DOUGLAS: You've spoiled it for me, Barbara.
    I shall never come here and look at all
    this the same way again ever;
    and I used to come here often, two three
    times a year
    and never worry about anything,
    never look at anything too closely,
    now you've seen in and I'm lost,
    it's real,
    you've made me look at it and I'm
    terrified... and I've always enjoyed
    coming here, a couple of nights
    a lot of talk about movies that will never
    be made,
    we all know they're not going to get made...
    that's half the fun of it. It only goes
    wrong when you care.
    It's only a fucking film, Barbara. That's
    all. Now –
    what did I say I'd do Barbara?

    For the nice policeman, Barbara?

BARBARA: I don't know. Don't blame me. You've
    spoiled it for me, Douglas.

    I knew I shouldn't have come.

DOUGLAS: No no, I wouldn't have come without you.
    I rely on you.

BARBARA: I don't think that's good enough.

DOUGLAS: Yes it is. It is for me.

What was I like before?

BARBARA: Before what?

DOUGLAS: Before you knew me.

BARBARA: I didn't know you before I knew you.

DOUGLAS: Nonsense, you've always known me.

BARBARA: No I haven't.

DOUGLAS: And you always will. I know what I'll do.
I'll give him his orgy. Wow!

Oh, I'm not good at love, Barbara.

BARBARA: Yes you are, you never mention it.

He took more easily to colour when it
came, Douglas,
something else to hide behind.
I'm still black and white,
not brothels,
not prostitutes and police calls,
but real pictures, black and white in
the Garden of Allah.

Myrna Loy in a house of ill fame.

I'll not forgive him for bringing me
here, Douglas.
I hate what he does.
I hate them down there, and up there
offering their bodies, fluttering their names.
I hate him for bringing me here all this way
and then not opening the door,
standing me on the edge when I'm too far
gone to fly.

I hate my life for it not being a movie. I
hate not being in the picture.

If he didn't do it I wouldn't know I was
only in the bloody rewrites.

DOUGLAS: Barbara. Do you realise we have lived
together more years than we haven't.
There isn't anything after you, or after
me, for us, we defy Rutherford. We
can't be split. We're fused.

BARBARA: Should I die, Douglas, promise me at least,
don't let me be buried here.

The curtain falls.

THE END